By
Carol Mader

Loveland, Colorado

Crazy Clothesline Characters

Visit our Web site: **www.grouppublishing.com**

CREDITS
Editor: Linda A. Anderson
Creative Development Editor: Jim Kochenburger
Chief Creative Officer: Joani Schultz
Copy Editor: Shirley Michaels
Art Director: Jean Bruns
Illustrator: Victoria Hummel
Cover Art Director: Jeff A. Storm
Cover Design: Ellen Bruss Design
Cover Illustration: David Merrell
Computer Graphic Artist: Nighthawk Design, Tracy K. Donaldson
Production Manager: Peggy Naylor

Library of Congress Cataloging-in-Publication Data
Mader, Carol.
Crazy clothesline characters / by Carol Mader.
p. cm.
ISBN 0-7644-2140-9
1. Bible stories--Study and teaching. 2. Christian education--Teaching methods. I. Title.
BS546.M26 2000
268'.6--dc21 99-17016
CIP

10 9 8 7 6 5 4 3 2 1 09 08 07 06 05 04 03 02 01 00

Printed in the United States of America.

CONTENTS

Old Testament Stories

CONTENTS

continued

New Testament Stories

INTRODUCTION

Like Lazarus lying silent in his tomb waiting to be called to life, Bible stories lie dormant within the pages of Scripture awaiting liberation. God's Word sizzles with tales of passionate love, savage hate, and desperate fright. The Bible is bursting with intoxicating adventures told from the heights of mountains to the depths of a whale's belly. Manic-depressive kings, heartbroken fathers, jealous wives, and stubborn prophets permeate the pages of Scripture as a mirror into our modern-day souls. How can we do justice to these tales of tragedy and triumph? How can we teach such captivating stories to our children in a way that touches them? Now we can share our enthusiasm for God's Word in creative ways.

Whether you teach Sunday school, children's church, midweek club or your children at home, the Bible story is central, the heartbeat of teaching God's Word. *Crazy Clothesline Characters* is a tool for you to share God's Word in an exciting way and a springboard to teach you how to soar into your own imagination. You can incorporate this book into your current curriculum or use each story as a weekly lesson, complete with extension ideas. Some poetic license has been taken in interpreting God's Word for children. Please read the original passage in your Bible before sharing the stories with your class. Prepare with prayer and a life that lives God's Word. He promises to return his Word with a full harvest (Isaiah 55:10-11).

Hebrews 4:12 tells us that the Word of God is living and active. Yet how have we told the Bible stories to our children? By telling them to sit still and listen! The techniques outlined in this book were designed from a child's point of view. We've incorporated children's senses, cognitive development, and energy to touch their emotions so children will remember.

It's my privilege and joy to share these stories and techniques so that you may share them with your children. Variety is the spice of life, so let's get shaking! When object lessons lose their luster and flannel graphs fatigue, open these pages to discover creative new ways to tell that wonderful Bible story. May God use this book as a sword in your hand to sharpen a lackluster presentation, vitalize your ministry, and breathe fresh life into Bible adventures for the children's sake.

Yours for making the teaching about God our Savior vital (Titus 2:10).

Carol Mader

ACKNOWLEDGEMENTS

Every book is a reflection of the author. Each author is a composite image of the people who touch our lives. With special love and thanks to the following people who have touched my life and been a part of this book:

- My dad and especially my mom who nurtured a creative spirit in our family.
- My husband for his financial support. It would have been tough without you.
- My own boys, Ivan and Hans, for sharing their mom with a computer.
- Lori Niles whose keen eye originally caught the vision for this book.
- My kindred spirit, Celeste Johnson, who is always willing to hear my crazy ideas.
- Gary L. Thomas whose own profound Bible stories freed me to actually write this book. Thank you.
- My church family at Wall Highway Baptist Church and especially Cindy Kosanda for the encouragement.
- John Rankin who was so willing to share from his astoundingly deep well of Biblical knowledge.
- My friends who helped with my children, especially Nan Taylor, Beth Matthis, Angie Johnson, and Karen Pamfilis.
- My extended family at Group Publishing. Finding Group was like coming home.
- My terrific, talented, new editor Linda Anderson. What a joy it's been to team up with you. Thanks for your work and enthusiasm!
- May all the excitement this book produces go to my Lord Jesus Christ. When I was weak, he made me strong. All things are possible only through him.

Old Testament Stories

K-1

Mystery Containers

Create some Creation elation! This interactive story is packed with sensory experiences that young learners crave! The days of Creation are illustrated with objects from nature that are hidden in empty oatmeal containers. These mystery containers entice children to reach in, feel, and guess what God made on each day. Since tactile experiences promote learning, this technique is tops for touching!

The Story

Creation, Genesis 1–2:1-2

The Point

God's creation is a special gift.

The Materials

Seven empty oatmeal or snack containers, black spray paint, black fabric, duct tape, a flashlight, an empty plastic zipper bag, a jar of water, a plastic zipper bag of sand, a plastic zipper bag of potting soil, a flower or leaves, an apple, a knife, glow-in-the-dark stars and planets, craft feathers, a bag of fish-shaped crackers, miniature plastic animals, a small doll, a scrap of soft fabric, a pan, and a Bible.

Preparation

Wipe out the empty oatmeal containers with a damp cloth. If you can't acquire enough containers, just use paper grocery sacks. If you spray paint these containers black and add a bit of black fabric to the opening, you'll create an ambiance of intrigue. Cut the fabric to the size of the opening of the containers. Use duct tape on the inside of the containers to attach the fabric so it forms a curtain over the opening. After your containers are prepared and labeled as Day 1, Day 2, and so on, fill the containers with the following:

DAY	CREATION	OBJECT REPRESENTATION
Day 1	the light	a flashlight
Day 2	the sky	resealable plastic bag, filled with air
Day 3	water, land, plants	jar of water, bags of sand and soil, flower or leaves, apple (Have the pan nearby.)

Day 4	sun, moon, stars	glow-in-the-dark stars and planets *
Day 5	birds, fish	feathers, fish-shaped crackers
Day 6	animals and man	miniature plastic animals and a doll**
Day 7	God rested	a piece of fabric

*If you can't find these in a department store, you can cut out some star shapes and color them with a fluorescent crayon or paint. You may want to put some putty in the container to hang the stars on the wall later.

**If you can't find a miniature human doll, you can use a small mirror to represent the people God made.

Let's Begin

(Gather the children on the floor around you. Have the containers in a box or bag where the children can't see them. Open your Bible to Genesis 1.) This is the first book of the Bible; it's called the book of Genesis. This amazing book tells us how our world began! We can know what happened thousands of years ago, before there was one man or woman on the earth, because God tells us. You are going to help me tell the story of the creation of the world.

(Turn the lights off so the room is mostly dark.) In the beginning of time, the earth was empty and dark. Everything, everywhere was completely dark *(Whisper.)* and probably completely silent. Let's be perfectly still and quiet for a moment. You can close your eyes if you want.

With just four words, God wiped out the darkness! He said, "Let there be...*(Let a child reach into the first container and the pull out the flashlight.)*...LIGHT!" And there was. *(Help a child turn on the flashlight.)* A warm, bright glow chased away all the shadows. *(Turn on the classroom lights.)* God called the light "day," and the darkness he called...*(Let the kids guess.)* "night." And so God created the very first day.

The earth was covered with water. God's spirit floated over it. Can you breathe under water? There is no air. God knew the living things he would create would need air, so on the second day, God separated the water below from water above. God said, "Let there be...*(Let a child reach in and find bag of air.)*...a space in the middle of the water. And it was so." The space in between was called "sky." God created air and sky—the atmosphere. Take a deep breath. Now let it out. Isn't it great to breathe? God was preparing the earth for the rest of his creation.

On the third day, God said, "Let the...*(Let a child reach in and pull out the jar of water.)* ... water on the earth be gathered into one place, and let...*(Have a child pull out a bag of sand and the bag of soil.)*...dry ground appear." And it was so. *(Put the sand in the pan. Cover it with the water from the jar. Let the children take turns tilting the pan so that the "dry ground" can appear.)* God created land and our oceans. And God saw that it was **good**.

On this same day, God created plants and trees with fruit on them. Mmmm. *(Have a child reach in and pull out the flower or leaf. Also, pull out the apple. Cut it in half, and let the children look at the seeds. Cut the apple into enough pieces for each child to have one. Pass out pieces of the apple for the kids to munch on while you continue the story.)* After God created the salty seas, the lovely land, and the leafy plants, God said that it was **good.**

On the fourth day, God said, "Let there be lights in the sky." And it was so. God made one light to rule the day. It is a burning ball of light and heat. Do you know what it is? *(Let one or more children reach in and pull out the glow-in-the-dark stars and moon and sun. Hold up the sun.)* It is called the sun. He made another light to rule the night. It is called the...moon. *(Hold up the moon.)* God made millions of dazzling stars and scattered them across the universe. And God saw that what he had made was...**good!** *(Hang the stars and sun and moon up with putty, and turn out the lights. Most glow-in-the-dark materials work best after being exposed to fluorescent lights.)*

On the fifth day, God said, "Let the water be filled with living creatures, and let birds fly above the earth across the sky." *(Let a child reach in and pull out the feathers and another, the fish crackers.)* And it was so. The seas were full of fish splashing and dolphins playing in the waves. The sky was filled with colorful birds catching the breeze on their feathers. God saw that what he made was...**good.** *(Allow the children to eat some of the fish crackers.)*

On the sixth day, God said, "Let living creatures come forth." *(Let one or more children reach in and pull out the plastic miniature animals.)* And it was so. God made the animals! *(Allow the children to briefly act out these motions.)* Some slithered, and some bounced. Some hopped, and some pounced. Some purred, and some had fur. Some howled, and some growled. He made big animals that pound the ground and tiny ones that creep around. God shows us his wonderful imagination by the amazing animals he made. And God saw that it was...**good!**

Now the earth was ready. God had prepared the world for the very best of his creation. He had made light to see, air to breathe, and food growing on the trees. God had made silky sand, green grass, the warm sun, and animals waiting to be petted. The earth was clean, fresh, and ready. God said, "Let us make man in our likeness." And so God created...*(Let a child reach in and pull out the doll.)*...man and then woman to be like him in many ways. Adam, the first man, was formed out of the dust of the earth. Adam lay on the ground like a still puppet. And God breathed into man the breath of life, and man became a living being. Adam opened his eyes. He sat up. He looked at the world around him. He smiled. God smiled too. God saw all that he made, and guess what? It was **very good.**

On the seventh day, God...*(Have a child reach in and pull out the material. Touch it to your face and close your eyes.)*...rested. And God blessed the seventh day and made it special because he rested on that day. He had created an awesome world. God sat back with a smile to enjoy his creation.

Questions

- Tell about the best gift you have ever gotten.
- How do you feel when you get a very special gift?
- How is God's creation like a special gift?
- What can you do to take care of the earth God made?

Story Extension Ideas

- Put the objects in a pile in the center of the room, and see if the children can retell the story putting the items in the correct containers.
- Have the children use objects from the story to make their own Creation books.
- Let the kids fill in the blank space in the poem by acting out something God created.

God is awesome.
His creation is good!
God made ________________.
Only God could!

Other Story Possibilities

Use Mystery Containers to tell other Bible stories that revolve around that special number, seven.

- David is anointed. 1 Samuel 16:1-13. Put a flannel graph figure of a man in each container. Read the story of Jesse's sons. (See also 1 Chronicles 2:13-15.) Let the kids pull out the figures as Eliab, Abinadab, Shammah, and the other brothers pass before Samuel. Bring David out, and remind the children of 1 Samuel 16:7: The Lord looks at the heart.
- Teach older children about the seven churches in Revelation 1–3. Hide objects to represent the churches: Ephesus—a candle to represent a lampstand; Smyrna—a crown or chains; Pergamum—a sword and a white stone; Thyatira—broken pottery; Sardis—a dirty cloth; Philadelphia—an open door made out of cardboard; and Laodicea—a jar of lukewarm water. Let the kids find the hidden object and symbolism.

K-1

Rainbow of Colors

This simple technique requires little preparation and is effective to use with a large group. Tell the story by handing children each a different sheet of colored paper and having them stand up and sit back down whenever the color they hold is named.

The Story

Noah's Ark, Genesis 6–9

The Point

God's promises are special.

The Materials

Sheets of 8½x11 paper in the following colors: red, orange, yellow, gold, green, blue, purple, white, black, brown, and tan. Have enough for each child to have a sheet. You will also need one sheet of each color for the teacher, arranged in the order of the rainbow. This paper, purchased at a copy store, is usually brighter than construction paper and can be purchased individually.

Preparation

You may want to use crayons to underline the color words in the story with the corresponding color. Have the colors of the rainbow set aside, ready to display.

Directions

Hand children each a color, and let them stand up and sit back down when their color is called.

Let's Begin

God made our world full of a rainbow of colors. I'm going to tell you a story full of a rainbow of colors. In the story, whenever you hear the name of the color of the paper that you are holding, stand up. Sit down when a color is said that is not the one you are holding.

Just after God made the world, people lived for about eight hundred years! That gave them a chance to do a lot of good. Unfortunately, that also gave them a chance to do a lot of…bad. The Lord saw that men and women had become wicked. He could look into their hearts that were filled with sin. The Lord was sad that he had made people. His **red** heart was broken.

The Lord said, "I will wipe mankind from the

face of the earth—men, women, and animals." But one man had a **red** heart that was still pure. It was…Noah. Noah walked with God. He obeyed God and tried to please him. God said to Noah, "I am going to put an end to all people—**tan, brown,** and **black**—because they are hurting and killing each other. But not you, Noah. So I want you to make an ark out of **brown** cypress wood. Make rooms in it, and cover it with **black** tar to keep the water out. Make a roof and a door. I am going to cause **blue** water to cover all of the earth to destroy all life, every creature that has breath in it. But I will make a special promise to you and your family: I will save you and two of every kind of animal. Store food on your ark for you, your family, and the animals."

Noah did everything just as God had commanded him, even though he was six hundred years old. While he built the ark, Noah thought about how much God loved the people and animals he had made and how awful it would be for God to destroy it all.

Noah finished the ark and filled it with food: **red**, juicy apples for the **brown** horses; **golden** hay for the **black** and **white** cows; **green** plants for the **gray** elephants; **pink** shrimp for the **pink** flamingos; and lots of **yellow** bananas for the hairy, **brown** monkeys.

Then the animals came creeping, strutting, flying, and pounding out of woods, fields, ponds, and trees. Noah's ark became filled with **orange** orangutans, **purple** peacocks, **green** grasshoppers, and bright **yellow** canaries. The ark creaked under the weight of hippos that were **gray**, jaguars that were spotted **gold** and **black**, and egrets that were snowy **white**. Even butterflies whose wings were swirled with **purple** and **red** hitched a ride on board. Noah and his family entered the ark. God was ready. The Lord himself shut the door of the ark.

The rain began. Floods of **blue** water covered the earth. For forty days the flood kept rising, the rain kept falling, and the waters grew higher and higher, covering all the animals, people, and plants on the whole earth, drowning everything. Even the highest mountains were covered with water. Every living thing on the face of the earth was wiped out. Only Noah and those with him in the ark stayed alive.

The ark floated for almost a year. The animals on board were growing restless. The people on board were getting impatient, and the food was starting to run out. But God remembered Noah. He sent a wind to blow back all the waters. Finally, the ark landed on the peak of a mountain, and God said to Noah, "Come out of the ark!"

Golden lions roared and sprang down the plank. **Green** gators growled and crawled, splashing into the water. **Orange**-billed toucans shrieked with joy as they stretched their wings and disappeared over the horizon. **Brown** kangaroos bounced with their babies into the fresh air. Tiny **red** and **black** ladybugs crept and then buzzed their way into the new world.

When Noah and his family came out of the ark, they gasped. An eerie silence greeted them. There were probably no sounds of children laughing or hammers pounding. I imagine the world was **gray**. Rocks were thrown around everywhere; huge trees were ripped down and floating on the water. A raw chill swept over the family.

But as they stood there, feeling so little and lonely, something amazing happened in the sky. Colors! A huge bending smile of colors glowed in the sky—*(Fan out these colors in your hand.)* **red, orange, yellow, green, blue, indigo and purple.** It was like an upside-down smile from God. He said, "Whenever you see a rainbow in the sky, it is my promise to you that I will never again flood the earth. I will remember my promise to you."

And God has kept that promise. So the next time you are lucky enough to see a rainbow glittering in the sky, you'll remember it as a promise and a smile from the God who loves you.

Questions

- Turn to the person next to you and smile. How do you feel when someone smiles at you?
- How do you think Noah and his family felt when they saw God's "color-smile" in the sky?
- What else does God promise us in the Bible?
- Is there a promise you'd like to make to God?

Story Extension Ideas

- Let the kids make booklets and retell the story themselves. Draw vertical and horizontal lines on the colored papers every two inches to form twenty two-inch squares. Let each child cut up one page of a different color. The children can share the squares until they each have one square of each color. Let them punch holes in the corners and slip a colorful paper clip through. Now the children have their own rainbow-colored books.
- Teach the kids this poem. They can paint a rainbow as you recite it.

A rainbow is a promise,
A promise from above.
A rainbow is a promise
Of God's unending love.
The red reminds me of his heart,
That was broken all apart.
An orange sun set on the last day
Before all life was swept away.
The yellow tells me of the sun
God shone again on everyone.
The green plants grew,
The sky was blue,
Purple flowers, all the hues.
God's rainbow stretches for a mile.
A rainbow is his big, wide smile.

Other Story Possibilities

You can tell many Bible stories with colors and some imagination.

- Tell the story of the wise men visiting Jesus with their robes of purple and gifts of gold. The brilliant white star could be cut like a snowflake as you are telling about it. See Matthew 2.
- A Creation account would be very easy to translate into colors from Genesis 1. The children could even select their own colors to describe the fresh, new world filled with a spectrum of hues of animals and flowers.

2-3

Tower Power

There's power in a story tower! Children in grades two and three will build a story fort out of index cards. As the teacher reads the story, the children look at their index cards for key words. If they hold a key word card, they can add it to the story fort. Watch the reality of the story grow as the tower grows before the children's eyes.

The Story

Tower of Babel, Genesis 11:1-9

The Point

We must remember to honor God.

The Materials

For each child: pencil, scissors, and at least three small index cards

Preparation

Make a practice tower yourself so you know how to help the kids.

Directions

Hand out at least three cards to each child. Show the kids how to cut their cards. Holding the cards with the long edges at the top and bottom, have them cut notches in their cards about one inch from the left edge and one-half inch into the card on the top and bottom. This technique is quite forgiving, so don't worry if their measurements aren't accurate. Go through the story, and assign the key words that are printed in bold. Each key word will have its own card. The children each will write different key words on their own cards. The number of words each child will have will depend on the size of your class. If you have a large class, add some other words from the story. You may write out the key words on the cards ahead of time if you want to save time.

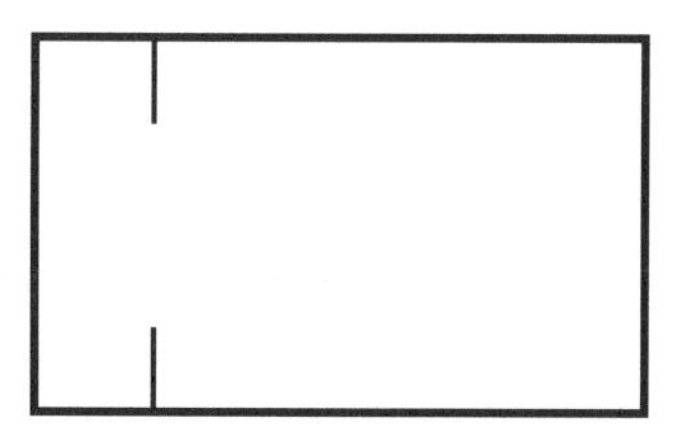

As you read the story, ask the children to listen closely for their key words. When you say a key word, that child will quietly come up and add his or her card to the story fort. Children can wiggle the cards into position in whatever way the cards will fit. Can you tell the whole story before the fort collapses?

Let's Begin

(*Open your Bible to Genesis 11.*) Chapter 11 in the book of Genesis in the **Bible** tells about a tower named **Babel**. It tells how the language of the people got scrambled and they started to babble! After the flood, Noah and his family were the only survivors. They banded together and set to work building their homes. They had **children**. And their children had children—lots of children. They formed **communities** and moved, settling in Shinar, a plain between two mighty rivers.

At that time, the whole world had only one **language**. The people could **understand** each other easily, as we can today. Since the people lived for hundreds of years back then, they became very **smart**.

They said to each other, "Come, let's make **bricks** and bake them." Then they said, "Come, let **us** build ourselves a city, with a **tower** that reaches to the **heavens**, so that we may make a **name** for **ourselves** and not be scattered over the face of the whole earth."

Did you hear that? Why might they have wanted to build a tower? They built the tower to build a name for **themselves**. Here, the word "name" means "renown." That means the people of Babel wanted to be **famous** and have people everywhere **honor** them. Uh-oh. God doesn't like that kind of **attitude**. That's like stealing from God.

The people started their tower. They spent hour after hour packing **mud** and **straw** into ovens to bake the bricks. They spent hour after hour shoveling black, sticky **tar** to keep the bricks together. They spent hour after hour hauling those heavy bricks up, up, up the tower. It **grew**.

As the tower grew, so did their **pride**. "Look at what we can do! Aren't we smart and **strong** and wonderful?"

But the Lord came down to see the city and the tower that the men were building. He was not **impressed**. The Lord said, "If as one people speaking the same language they have begun to do this, then **nothing** they plan to do will be impossible for them." Now, God could have simply zapped their tower. Or he could have simply zapped the people. But he didn't. He had a different **plan**. He said, "Come, let us go down and **confuse** their language so they will not understand each other."

And that's exactly what happened. One day, as they were pulling a brick out of the oven, one man might have said, "Hey, hand me that hot mitt."

But the other man heard him say, "**Mephibo lito basha**."

When he tried to say back, "What did you say?" it came out as "**Zo riminy bo biminy**?"

The men looked at each other, startled. When the tar was being unloaded and one man asked another to throw him a rope, it came out as, "**Yahoo la slahoo**." Pretty soon the whole city was in an **uproar**. There was enough **confusion** to start a revolution.

God's plan worked. The people put down their bricks and went to find other people that spoke their same new language. They made groups. These groups moved to other places. So the Lord scattered them from there over the whole earth. And they **stopped** building the city. The tower was called Babel (which means confusion) because there the Lord confused the language of the whole world. And the tower was never **finished**.

Questions

- How did you feel as our tower grew?
- How did the people of Babel feel about themselves as their tower grew?
- How does God feel when people decide to honor themselves rather than him?
- Can you share a time when you felt proud of something you did?
- When you do something special, how can you give God the glory?

Story Extension Ideas

- Let each child make a brick out of clay or plaster of Paris, using disposable aluminum loaf pans. Then use a permanent marker to write Isaiah 26:8b ("Your name and renown are the desire of our hearts.") on each brick. Use putty to keep the bricks together as a class conversation piece.
- Teach each child a few phrases in another language, and have the children try to communicate with each other. Then invite three people who speak other languages to come into your classroom and pray aloud in the foreign tongues.

Other Story Possibilities

- Compare the kingdoms that Uzziah and Jotham built. Build a sturdy tower out of Jotham's story. He grew powerful because he walked steadfastly with the Lord (2 Chronicles 27:6). King Uzziah became powerful also, but his pride led to his downfall (2 Chronicles 26:16). Let Uzziah's tower collapse.
- Tell the story of rebuilding the walls of Jerusalem from the book of Nehemiah, particularly the first two chapters. Teach the children how prayer is the foundation for any task they set out to accomplish.

4-5

Mask-arade

Many tribes in Africa use ceremonial masks to tell stories about their ancestors. The children will listen to clues as the story is told and select the correct satirical mask to join in the storytelling. This Mask-arade parade tells the fascinating history of Israel's family heritage.

The Story

The Twelve Tribes, Genesis 29:18-30–30:24, 35:16-18, 23-26

The Point

Good can come from bad circumstances.

Materials

Twelve plastic foam plates, photocopies of the "Baby Faces" handout (pp. 19-20), scissors, glue, a knife, yarn, a marker, paper for signs, and a stapler

Preparation

Photocopy the faces, enlarging them to fit the plates. Cut out the pictures of the baby faces, and glue each one to a plate. (If you want to make it into a real mask, cut out the eyes, too. Then after you've glued the face to the plate, use a knife to make holes for the eyes.) Write the name of the tribe on the back of the mask so the children can't see it. Make signs that say "Rachel" and "Leah," and place them on opposite sides of the room. Also make signs for the name of each son and for the meaning of each name. Have them in a pile near the masks.

Directions

Place the masks against a wall or propped up on the tray of a chalkboard. Have the children form a row and sit down. While you tell the story, direct one child at a time to come up to the table and select a mask according to the clues given about the baby's name, along with the correct name and meaning. The child picks up the mask, holds it in front of his or her face, and moves to the area labeled either "Rachel" or "Leah," depending on who was the mother of the person depicted by the mask. Following are the names and meanings used in the story: Reuben, "look, a son"; Simeon, "one who hears"; Levi, "joined in harmony"; Judah, "praise"; Dan, "vindicated"; Naphtali, "my struggle"; Gad, "good fortune"; Asher, "happy"; Issachar, "reward"; Zebulun, "honor"; Joseph, "may he add"; and Benjamin, "son of my right hand."

BABY FACES
ASHER
DAN
BENJAMIN
GAD
ISSACHAR
JOSEPH

LEVI
JUDAH
NAPHTALI
SIMEON
REUBEN
ZEBULUN

Let's Begin

Jacob picked up Rachel and swung her around. Her black hair flew into her eyes, but she laughed. "We can finally be married!" Jacob said as he placed Rachel on the ground and kissed her.

"I can't believe we've waited seven years," Rachel said, hugging Jacob.

"I love you so much that it seems like only a few days," Jacob said.

Rachel hurried off to get dressed in her wedding gown. When Jacob came out to meet his bride, she was wearing a beautiful white gown. Her face was covered with a veil. She wore her finest jewelry and a wreath of flowers upon her head. That night, in the light of blazing torches, the wedding guests celebrated with roasted lamb, wine, dancing, and music. Later, after the guests had all left, Jacob took his new bride into his tent.

The next morning, Jacob pulled back the covers to give Rachel a kiss. He gasped, "You aren't Rachel! You're Leah, Rachel's sister! What a wicked trick!"

Leah only gave a weak, embarrassed smile and said, "Do you think you could learn to love me?"

Jacob stormed out of the tent to Leah and Rachel's father, Laban. "What is this you have done to me? I worked seven years for you for Rachel, not Leah!"

"You know we have a tradition of marrying the oldest daughter first," Laban answered. "You can have Rachel, too, but you must work for me another seven years." And that is how Jacob ended up with two wives.

But Jacob loved Rachel more. When the Lord saw that Leah was not loved, he gave Leah a son. She named him **Reuben**. The name Reuben means, "Look, a son," and sounds like the word for "he has seen my misery." Leah thought, Surely my husband will love me now.

She had another baby boy and named him **Simeon**, which means "one who hears." She said, "I named him this because the Lord heard that I am not loved and so he gave me this son, too."

Leah gave birth to another son and said, "Now at last my husband will feel joined to me because I have given him three sons." So she named him **Levi**, which means "joined in harmony." But Jacob still loved Rachel more.

When Leah had another baby boy, she named him **Judah**, which means "praise." She said, "This time I will praise the Lord." Then she stopped having children.

Rachel saw her sister's arms filled with babies and watched little boys scamper happily about. Her own arms felt empty. Jealousy burned within her. She said to Jacob, "Give me children, or I'll die!"

Jacob became angry and said, "Am I God? I can't help it if you aren't having children." And so Jacob used Rachel's maidservant like a wife. The servant had a baby for Rachel. Rachel named him **Dan**, which means "vindicated" or "made right." She thought, "Now that I have a baby, things are made right."

Rachel had another son this way and named him **Naphtali**, which means "my struggle." When she handed Jacob the squiggling baby, she told him, "I named him Naphtali because I've had a great struggle with my sister and won!"

Leah did the same thing with her maidservant. That baby was named **Gad**, which means "good fortune."

Another son came this same way, and Leah named him **Asher**, which means "happy." She said, "How happy I am! All the women will call me happy."

The crazy race went on. Leah had still another son and named him **Issachar**, which sounds like the Hebrew word for "reward." She felt like the Lord rewarded her with yet another son.

Oh, yes, Leah had another baby boy and named him **Zebulun**, which means "honor." "God has presented me with a precious gift. This time my husband will treat me with honor, because I have given him six sons!" She even had a girl named Dinah.

But God had not forgotten Rachel. She finally gave birth to her very own baby boy and named him **Joseph**, which means "may the Lord add." She said, "May the Lord add to me another son."

And God did. But while Rachel was giving birth, she had great difficulty—in fact, she was dying. As she breathed her last breath, she named her son Ben-Oni, which means "son of my trouble." But his father named him **Benjamin**, which means "son of my right hand." In those days the people thought the right hand was the best. Sadly, Rachel died. Jacob's name changed too—to Israel.

And so that is how Israel had twelve sons. The twelve sons had their own families, and those families had families. They called their families "tribes." The tribes settled land and became their own countries. They became the Jewish nation, the light of the world, the apple of God's eye, and his very own earthly family.

Questions

- How do you think Leah and Rachel felt about the situation they were in?
- God used this problem situation and started the twelve tribes of Israel. Can you share about a time when God took a bad situation in your life and turned it into good?
- What can you do the next time you are in a situation that seems bad?

Story Extension Ideas

- Bring in a baby name book. Let the kids each look up the meaning of their own name and tie it to a Scripture verse. Show them how to use a concordance to do this. For example, the name "Briana" means "strong." You could use the verse from Psalm 24:8 "The Lord strong and mighty." Use your best handwriting to write each child's name and its meaning on a sheet of colored paper.
- Make a map of the twelve tribes and the land they settled. Let the kids color in their own tribe. Talk about God's promises coming true.

Other Story Possibilities

- Make masks of the good and bad kings of Judah and Israel, using lots of craft jewelry. Have each child share one story about his or her king. Look through the books of 1 and 2 Samuel, 1 and 2 Kings and 1 and 2 Chronicles.
- Matthew 25 tells the parable of the ten virgins. Have the kids make masks of the women and use flashlights to act out the dramatic arrival of the bridegroom. Use real fabric for their headdresses.

K-1

Imagination Stations

This lively technique allows children to experience the story while traveling from station to station. The children become part of the story in this active, personalized drama.

The Story

Joseph, Genesis 37, 39–41

The Point

God has a plan for everyone.

The Materials

Bathrobe, three colors of streamers, masking tape, markers, nickels or dimes for each child, cups for each child, unpopped popcorn kernels in a large bowl, a large container, small plastic stars for each child, and a sheet to hang for a tent

Preparation

Set up the following areas in your room. Station 1: Place the plastic stars on the floor. Station 2: Set out streamers and tape, and hang a sheet to make a tent. Station 3: Arrange chairs in a circle to form a small "pit". Station 4: Set up two tables so children may pass between them and sit on the other side. Make signs as described below for each area. Read through the story at least once before doing this with the children.

Directions

Follow the directions in parentheses. Use a deep, angry voice for the brothers' words. Lead the children; have them sit at each station as the story indicates.

Let's Begin

STATION 1: THE PASTURE

(Put on the robe.) I'll be Joseph, and you can be his brothers. Joseph, his eleven brothers, and their father, Jacob, lived long ago, after Abraham and before Moses. Now Joseph had ten older brothers and one younger brother. They were Reuben, Simeon, Levi, Judah, Issachar, Zebulun, Dan, Naphtali, Gad, Asher, and Benjamin. The father seemed to like Joseph the best. Joseph listened when his father, Jacob, talked about God's plans.

One day, when Joseph was seventeen years old, he was tending the flocks with his brothers. One of them had an idea, a bad idea. The Bible doesn't say what the bad idea was. Joseph left his brothers to go to Jacob's tent.

STATION 2: JACOB'S TENT

"Father, I have something bad I have to tell you," Joseph said.

"What is it?" his father asked.

"My brothers are not doing a good job for you."

Jacob called the brothers home from the field and scolded them. *(Shake your finger.)*

STATION 1: THE PASTURE

Later, out in the pasture, how do you think the brothers felt about Joseph? *(Let the children respond.)* They hated him!

"That little tattle-tale," growled Issachar.

"He always thinks he so perfect," said Naphtali.

"I hate him," said Dan.

"Me too," his other brothers said. *(Have the kids cross their arms and growl, and continue to make similar comments briefly.)*

STATION 2: JACOB'S TENT

Joseph was growing tall and strong. One day he said to his father, Jacob, "Dad, my coat doesn't fit anymore."

Jacob said, "I'll make you a new one, son. I'll make the finest robe you have ever seen. I'll make it all the colors of the rainbow."

"Wow, thanks, Dad," Joseph said.

(Tell the children you need their help to decorate a new robe for Joseph. Have the children each pick a color of streamer, tear it into two- to three-foot lengths, and tape it onto your robe. While they work, continue your story.)

Jacob went to work dying the wool, spinning it into thread, and weaving it on the loom. While he worked, the other brothers looked at their robes. Simeon said, "Look at my old blue robe I've had for years. Father never made me a fancy robe like that."

"Yeah," Asher said. "Look how my old brown robe is falling apart."

"I hate my dirty old robe too," Gad whined.

"I hate Joseph," said a very jealous Judah.

When Joseph's robe was finished, it was the most wonderful, colorful robe you ever saw. It made Joseph proud. But it made his brothers…mad.

"Look at Joseph prancing around in that ridiculous robe," complained Levi.

"It makes me sick to see him in it," Reuben said. "Dad must love Joseph more than all of us."

"I hate Joseph," said Asher.

"Me too," said all the brothers.

(Have the children fold their arms and growl and make similar comments.)

STATION 1: THE PASTURE

One day the brothers were out in the pasture when Joseph came up wearing his robe. The shining sun made the golden thread sparkle. Joseph said to them, "I had a dream! We were out in the field, tying our bundles of wheat together, when suddenly my bundle rose and stood upright. All of your bundles gathered around mine and bowed down to it."

(You may choose children to repeat these after you.)

Issachar said, "That's a stupid dream and you're stupid to tell it to us."

Naphtali leaned close to Joseph. His beard

tickled Joseph's smooth face. He hissed, "If you actually think you'll rule over us, you're crazy!"

"I wouldn't bow down to you if my life depended on it," Dan said.

"Hey, I can't help what I dream," Joseph said and went home.

"I hate him," Simeon said.

"Me too," the other brothers all said.

(Have the kids fold their arms and growl.)

Joseph later had a dream that the sun, moon, and eleven stars were bowing down to him. *(Hand each child a star.)* The brothers really hated him then. *(Let the kids throw their stars at the ground. Have them repeat the following line.)* "We'll never bow down to you," they said. *(Have them fold their hands and growl.)* Joseph's father thought to himself, Maybe God does have a plan for Joseph.

STATION 3: THE PIT

One day, the brothers saw Joseph coming as they were tending their flocks. The brothers said, "Here comes that dreamer. Let's kill him! Then we'll see what comes of his dreams!"

"Yeah, let's kill him," said the brothers.

"No, don't kill him," Reuben said. "Let's only throw him into this pit." Reuben was thinking that at night he would secretly rescue Joseph.

Joseph came up to his brothers. Before he could even say hello, they grabbed him. They stripped off his robe and threw him into the pit. *(Let the kids grab you, tear off your robe and pull you into the circle of chairs.)*

"Help! Let me out!" screamed Joseph. But his brothers just sat there eating their dinner. "Please, don't let me die down here," Joseph begged for his life.

"Look," Judah said. "Here come some men on their way to Egypt. Let's sell Joseph. He can be a slave and we'll get some money. Then we won't have to kill him."

Asher said, "Yeah, after all, he is our brother." So when the traders came by, his brothers pulled Joseph up out of the pit. They sold him for twenty pieces of silver. *(Let the kids pull you from the pit, and hand them each a nickel. Have one child hold you by the hand and lead you off to Egypt.)*

"Help, brothers! Don't do this to me! Help, dear Lord!"

Gad said, "Uh, guys, what are we going to tell Dad now?"

Simeon said, "Let's take his robe and dip it in blood. We'll pretend a wolf got him."

STATION 2: JACOB'S TENT

When the brothers showed the robe to their father, Jacob, he cried. He tore his clothes. He rocked back and forth weeping, "Joseph, my son. I'll go down to the grave weeping for my precious Joseph." His heart was broken. Jacob thought, How could this be God's plan?

STATION 4: EGYPT

Joseph was taken to Egypt. Questions raced through his mind. Where was he going? Who were these men? Why had his brothers been so mean? Would he ever see his father again? Why was God letting this happen to him? Could God really have a plan?

As Joseph came to Egypt, his eyes got wider and wider. He saw huge pyramids, bustling cities, and people with funny haircuts. He couldn't understand a word of their language. He was sold to a rich man and had to work as his slave. Some plan.

Joseph worked hard, and he did his work well. He learned to speak their language. Pretty soon he was in charge of the whole house. One day Joseph was taken before the king of Egypt, called the Pharaoh. Pharaoh had a dream that bothered him terribly. Joseph told the Pharaoh about the dream and God's plan. Joseph said, "Your dream means that we will have seven years with plenty of food and crops and then seven years without any rain or food. If I were you, I'd find a man to be in charge of storing the food away during the good years so you can survive through the bad years."

The Pharaoh was so amazed at Joseph's wise idea that he made Joseph an important leader in the country of Egypt! *(Tie some streamers around your head.)* He ruled the land and was second only to Pharaoh! God has amazing plans for those who trust and obey him—even a young Hebrew slave.

God's plan went into action. *(Hand the children cups and let them scoop up some popcorn kernels and pour them into one large container that you are holding.)* The people gave part of their food to Joseph, who saved it for them in big storehouses. When the good years were over, the clouds hung in the sky but wouldn't send down their rain. Crops died. People got hungry, even people in Canaan where Joseph's family was. But in Egypt, Joseph had food for everyone, because of his wise plan.

One day, Joseph's brothers came all the way to Egypt. They bowed before Joseph *(Have the kids all bow before you.)* and said, "Please give us some corn. We're hungry." Joseph remembered his dream from twenty-two years before. Joseph knew the men were his brothers, but they couldn't tell he was Joseph. He had grown up and looked like an Egyptian.

What could Joseph have done to his brothers? *(Let children respond.)* Did Joseph send them away without food? Did Joseph have them killed for what they did to him? Did Joseph scold them and say, "See, I told you so"? Joseph didn't do any of these things. He took off his headband *(Take off your headband.)* and said, "I am Joseph. You planned to hurt me, but God had a plan. I forgive you."

At first his brothers stood there, scared to death. But Joseph held open his arms and said, "Come to me." His brothers came to him, and they all hugged and kissed and cried. *(Open your arms, and let the children all come to you. Hug them.)* It was a very happy day. Joseph took care of his brothers and his father, too. God's plan worked! God had a plan for Joseph, and he has a good plan for you too!

Questions

- How do you think Joseph felt as he was being taken to Egypt as a slave?
- Tell about a time in your life when you might have felt as Joseph did then.
- How did Joseph feel at the end of the story when he was able to have food to feed his family and the country of Egypt?
- How can this story help you trust God when bad things happen in your life?

Story Extension Ideas

● Have the children write an "I forgive you" letter to someone who hurt them. Read them the story of the unforgiving servant in Matthew 18 and Colossians 3:13.

● Have the children make a time line of their lives, showing some things that might have seemed bad at the time but ended up being good and showing the blessings in their lives.

Other Story Possibilities

● Many stories can be told at stations when you use a little imagination. Paul and Silas in the prison is an exciting tale from Acts 16. Your stations will consist of the marketplace, prison, jailer's home, and lake where the family is baptized.

● Jesus walking on water (Mark 6:45-56) has action, drama, and adventure begging for the children to join in! They can follow Jesus from the hills where he is praying to the lake, into the boat, and then around Gennesaret.

2-5

Word Weavers

Two sheets of paper, scissors, and a Bible are all that are needed to weave a simple Bible story. Children cut one piece of paper into strips and weave it into another. Their curiosity and anticipation grow as the story takes shape. The children then read the story together from the words on the woven paper.

The Story

Baby Moses, Exodus 1–2:1-10

The Point

God has a plan.

The Materials

For each student: photocopies of the "Word Weaver" handout (p. 29-30), scissors, glue stick, and crayons

Preparation

Before class, practice making one of these yourself. Photocopy the two pages of text for each child.

Directions

Have the kids cut along the solid, then the dotted lines. They lay the page that reads "Exodus 1 and 2" down on top of the other page and weave each strip in and out so that every word shows. Have them glue each strip down after it is woven. When the whole story is woven, the class can read it aloud together. Let them color their weavings when they have finished the story.

For a greater challenge for fourth- and fifth-graders, have them weave the story and then flip it over. Let them dive directly into Scripture and try to tell the story of Moses as a baby in their own words in the blank squares. Once kids perfect this technique, they'll be eager to weave any story with their own words.

Let's Begin

(Lead the children in weaving their stories. Then read the story aloud.)

Moses was a Hebrew baby. The Egyptians tried to kill all the Hebrew babies. But God had a plan! Moses' mother wove a basket for him. She hid her baby in the basket so the Egyptians wouldn't find him. The basket floated down the Nile River. Pharaoh's daughter found Moses. She kept him. God's plans always work! Exodus 1–2.

WORD WEAVER

Moses Hebrew The tried

Hebrew But had Moses'

mother basket him. hid

basket Egyptians find The basket

floated the River. daughter

She him. plans work!

Exodus 1 & 2

WORD WEAVER
continued

	was a		baby.		Egyptians		to kill
all the		babies.		God		a plan!	
	wove a		for		She		her baby
in the		so the		wouldn't		him.	
	down		Nile		Pharaoh's		found
Moses.		kept		God's		always	

Questions

● How do you think Moses' mother felt when she placed her baby in the basket and put the basket into the river Nile?

● What was God's plan for Moses?

● How is God's care for us like his care for Moses?

● Can you share a time when God protected you?

Story Extension Ideas

● Talk about coincidence versus God's plans. (See Psalm 33:11.) Was it pure coincidence that Pharaoh's daughter just happened to be bathing in the Nile? that the soldiers never found Moses? that Pharaoh's daughter was sympathetic? Play this game to illustrate the fact that there is no such thing as coincidence in God's plan. Write down some Egyptian names, each one on its own card. The kids can make up their own. Include these names: Pharaoh's daughter, Shiphrah, Puah and some more modern day names like Aziza, Hida, Nabila, Ali, Nassir, Abdulla, and so on. They can repeat names to make more cards. On another set of cards, have the kids write Hebrew names. They can find plenty of these in their Bibles. Write "Moses" on one card. Have the children mix the Hebrew and Egyptian cards and then draw two out on each turn. How many times were Moses and Pharaoh's daughter matched?

● Talk about God's sense of humor in letting Moses' very own mother get paid for nursing her very own baby. Let the kids read other passages that reveal God's good nature, such as the story of the shrewd manager in Luke 16.

Other Story Possibilities

● Follow a similar weaving technique to create the coat of many colors (Genesis 37). Plan out a simple version of Joseph and his coat. Have the children weave colored strips of paper into a full sheet that has been cut into seven dangling strips. When the whole page has been woven and glued, the kids can cut it to look like Joseph's robe.

● The Bible is a book woven with words from many authors who were inspired by the Holy Spirit. Let the kids weave an 8½x17 paper to form a pattern of sixty-six squares. Children can fold it over and, on the inside left, write the books of Old Testament and, on the inside right, the books of the New Testament.

2-3

Memory-less Moses

This is a lot of fun for all ages and wonderful to use with a large group. The storyteller (Moses) pretends that he is so old that he can't remember all the details of the story. While the story is told, portions of it are described and left unfinished. The children are happy to come to the aid of the storyteller and thus become part of the storytelling.

The Story

The Plagues, Exodus 7–11

The Point

Keep our hearts "soft" towards God.

The Materials

A Biblical outfit, a walking stick, a long white beard. (A simple beard can be fashioned out of white wool material and yarn.)

Preparation

Prepare the outfit. Make an outline by highlighting key words in the script. This will allow you more eye contact. Underline each plague and the parts Moses forgets. Use your staff for motion and emphasis, pounding it on the ground as an attention-getter. You will need a helper for effects and to introduce you.

Directions

Seat the children quietly, and have your helper introduce you as a special guest as you hobble in. Use your best old man voice, and enjoy hamming it up for this tickle-the-funny-bone-tale.

Let's Begin

Hello, boys and girls. My name is…let's see; my name is…hmm. It starts with "M," and I took the Israelites out of Egypt across the Red Sea. My name is hmm…oh, yes…Moses. I'd like to tell you a story, but it all happened so long ago that sometimes I forget. If I forget, will you kids help me remember? Thanks.

Thousands of years ago, God's people were called the Israelites. See, the Israelites believed that God is real. That's why they were called the "Is-real-ites." Well, the Israelites, God's people, were—what do you call those people who get whipped and have to work hard without getting paid? Slaves! Yes, God's people were slaves in Egypt, and they cried out to God to free them. So God sent ME to the king of Egypt to say, "Let my people blow." No! "Let my people hoe." No? Oh, right…"Let my people GO!"

But Pharaoh snorted *(big snort)* and said, "No way. They're my slaves and they are not going anywhere. Besides, I'm the god around here."

So God told me to stretch out my hand across the river Nile. I did, and that river turned into—what's that red stuff that flows through your veins? Blood! Yes, the water in Egypt all turned to blood. The fish died and the river smelled awful. The Egyptians had to dig in the ground to get fresh water. You can't drink water that's been turned into a flood—I mean…blood.

I went back to Pharaoh and said, "Let my people crow. I mean…GO!" But Pharaoh said, "Blow…I mean No!" So God told my brother Aaron to stretch out the staff, and all of a sudden, Egypt was infested, covered with these jumpy little green amphibians called logs. No? Frogs! Right. Thanks. Ooh, those frogs were everywhere. There were slimy frogs in beds tickling our toes. Yuck! They were in the palace and even in the ovens. How would you like cooked frog for dinner? Pharaoh finally said he would let the Israelites go. All the frogs died. *(Hold your nose.)* Thousands of them were piled into heaps, and the land smelled awful! Pu-eey. But Pharaoh hardened his…*(Pound on your chest.)*…yes, thank you…his heart.

So God said, "Stretch out your staff and strike the ground. The dust of Egypt became ice—no, lice! The lice and gnats and mosquitoes crawled over the Egyptians. The lice swarmed in their hair, and they itched and scratched and itched and scratched! Ohh, itchy, itchy. It was awful! *(Scratch yourself.)* But Pharaoh hardened his mart—no, I mean his…heart.

So then God sent these…sticky, little black creatures that fly…lies? No, I'm not lying. I'm telling the truth! Oh, flies! Yes, God sent flies, millions of them. They swarmed into the Egyptians' homes. The flies swarmed everywhere, even up their noses. Ha, ha, ha. The Egyptians couldn't open their mouths without swallowing bunches of them. But the Israelites didn't get one fly in their homes.

The next plague was the death of all the livestock. That means all your helping animals, like the animals that go moo—yes, cows—and the those stubborn little animals that go hee-haw—donkeys—and even that huge animal called a box—no, an ox. Those fleecy, little animals that go baa—sleep—What's that? Oh, yes…sheep. They died too. You would think that all these troubles would soften Pharaoh's cart—no…heart. But it didn't. Pharaoh would not let the people mow…go.

And so God sent another plague. Boils, big red sores, broke out all over people's bodies so they hurt and itched. Did that soften Pharoah's part—heart? NO.

God was losing his patience. He said, "So you may know that there is no God like me in all the earth, I will send pail—no, tail—no—it's like frozen ice falling from the sky—That's it…hail. The smart Egyptians ran inside. The Lord sent thunder and lightning. *(Have your helper flash the lights.)* The lightning flashed all the way to the ground, and down came the hail. The hail killed every living thing outside—

the animals, crops and plants, even the people who were foolish enough to ignore God. The only place it didn't hail was in the land of the Israelites. But when the storm stopped, Pharaoh's heart again became card...hard.

God sent locusts next. They ate anything that was still alive and mean—I mean...green. Other Egyptians went to Pharaoh and said, "Let the people GO! Don't you realize yet that Egypt is ruined? Our beautiful lush country has turned into a wasteland!"

Did he? NO. So God sent plague number fine—I mean...nine. The entire land of Egypt became very, very...park—no...*(Have helper turn out the light.)*...dark. *(Whisper.)* The darkness became so deep and so dreadful you could reach out and feel it. But you couldn't see even your hand in front of your face. You could only hear the wails of the frightened children. Yet all the Israelites had light in their homes. *(Have your helper turn lights on again.)* Finally Pharaoh said, "OK, I will let the people go. But you must leave your cattle and flocks and herds behind. I said, "No way."

Pharaoh screamed, "Get out of my sight! If I see you again, you're dead."

I said, "Just as you say, but the Lord will bring about one more plague. *(Get very serious.)* At midnight, the Lord will send an angel of death throughout Egypt, and every firstborn male will die!" Would Pharaoh listen? No. His heart was hardened.

And so that night, the Israelites got ready. They killed a lamb and sprinkled the blood of the lamb over the door in their homes. God said that when he saw the blood he would pass over the house and not harm anyone in it. The blood would save them. But the Egyptians didn't listen to God. That night, the Egyptians woke up to screams and sobs. Every house had one dead person in it. Even Pharaoh's son had died. And so finally, finally Pharaoh said...GO. And we did. We left Egypt. It was a time of great miracles for us and great sorrow for the Egyptians. God showed that a proud, hardened heart can ruin everything.

Questions

- How did Pharaoh feel about God?
- How is this like having a "hard heart"?
- Talk with a partner about ways you can keep your heart from becoming hard.

Story Extension Ideas

- Have the kids make a heart out of modeling dough and paint it red. Set it on a paper plate that reads, "Let my people go? Pharaoh said 'no.' " Let it sit for a week to harden. Have the kids fill a resealable plastic bag with some modeling dough. On their bags, write with a permanent marker, "Make my heart fresh and new, moldable and soft for you."
- Research the gods of Egypt, and compare them with the plagues. God has distinct and fair reasons for everything he does. Hapi, the god of the Nile River, couldn't make the bloody water clean. The Egyptians worshipped the sun, cows, and insects. How did God obliterate their deities?

Other Story Possibilities

Almost any Bible story can be told "memory-less." Try to use the more familiar stories so the children will be successful in "helping" you out. Leave out key phrases or other portions of the text for the children to supply.

- Dress up as a Roman centurion who witnessed Jesus' death and resurrection in Matthew 26–28. You can tell the children that it was such a traumatic experience sometimes you forget the details.
- Have Samuel try to remember what his childhood days were like when he first went to live at the Temple (1 Samuel 1–2).

4-5

Sense-sational Stories

Touching a taste bud directly affects the brain, so teaching with food is smart! Jews use the Seder (pronounced say-dur) meal to tell the story of the Passover; Christians observe it during the Easter season. When children lick bitter herbs, taste salty tears and munch on a scorched egg, they remember the meaning behind the symbolism.

The Story

The Passover, Exodus 12

The Point

God sets us free!

The Materials

On each child's plate, place the following: two sprigs of parsley, bowl of saltwater, matzo bread, bitter herbs (use freshly grated horseradish or other bitter vegetables, such as romaine lettuce or onions), three small cups of juice, and haroset (a mixture of chopped apples, nuts, raisins, cinnamon, and grape juice). An extra plate as above is made for Elijah. Also make a plate for the leader, containing one bowl of saltwater, one lamb shank bone, one roasted egg, three whole squares of matzo crackers, and a small prize for the finder of the hidden matzo. Two white candles are optional but add to a meaningful ambiance. Be careful for fire safety. Try to use a nice tablecloth to add a special touch to the occasion.

Preparation

You may not need to visit a Jewish delicatessen; most of these items can be purchased in a grocery store. Prepare these at home ahead of time: Hard boil an egg, and then place it under a broiler until it browns. Get the lamb shank at a butcher's, and roast it as you did the egg. Let the children help you make the haroset. Set the places with an empty chair for Elijah.

Directions

This Haggadah (which means "narrative of the Passover") has been altered to recount the story while the meal takes place. After reading the Scripture passage, have the children eat (or at least taste) the food. You may ask the children to eat with sandals on, shirt tucked in, or wearing a jacket as a picture of eating in readiness to depart. (See Exodus 12:11.)

Let's Begin

Candles. The leader lights the candles saying, "Blessed are you, O Lord our God, King of the universe, who sanctifies us. You set us apart by your commandments. You have appointed us to celebrate the Passover."

Wine. With everyone seated, the leader lifts a cup of juice and reads Exodus 6:6-7 "Therefore, say to the Israelites: 'I am the Lord and I will bring you out from under the yoke of the Egyptians. I will free you from being slaves to them and I will redeem you with an outstretched arm and with mighty acts of judgment. I will take you as my own people, and I will be your God. Then you will know that I am the Lord your God...' " Everyone drinks a cup of juice.

Karpas. Dip some karpas (parsley) into saltwater. Explain that karpas stays green all year as a reminder of God's bounty, a symbol of new birth. Have everyone dip one sprig of parsley into saltwater and eat it. Explain that the saltwater is reminiscent of the Hebrews' tears while they cried out to God in their bondage. Read Exodus 3:7 when God spoke to Moses from the burning bush. "The Lord said, 'I have indeed seen the misery of my people in Egypt. I have heard them crying out because of their slave drivers, and I am concerned about their suffering. So I have come down to rescue them from the hand of the Egyptians...' "

Maros. These are the bitter herbs that are placed on a matzo and eaten. The herbs are a reminder of the suffering the Hebrews experienced in Egypt. Review highlights from the book of Exodus that describe the people's plight, including the slaughter of the firstborn sons, in Exodus 1 and Exodus 5:1-9.

Matzo. The leader breaks off a square of matzo and hides it while the children close their eyes.

Haroset. Each person puts some haroset on a matzo and eats it. The haroset represents the mortar that the Israelites used to make bricks. Read about how their plight was worsened when Pharoah forced the slaves to make bricks while gathering their own straw. Read Exodus 5:10-23.

Cup of plagues. God poured out plagues upon the Egyptians to show Pharaoh his mighty hand. Ask the children to recount the plagues for you, and then read about each plague aloud. After each plague is read, everyone dips a finger into his or her grape juice from the second cup and lets it fall onto the plate. Read about the first nine plagues in Exodus 7–10.

Lamb that saves. Review the Passover in Exodus 11-12. If you want to read only portions of this passage to save time, read Exodus 11 and Exodus 12:12-14, 21-36. Pass around the platter with the lamb shank on it.

Matzo. The children can eat the matzo and then search for the hidden matzo called the afikomen. The winner gets a small prize. Explain that this is unleavened bread, made without yeast to emphasize the Jews' hasty departure. See Exodus 12:39.

Karpos. While you tell the story of the parting of the Red Sea, dip the karpos in the saltwater. The saltwater is a reminder of the drowning of the Egyptian army. Read Exodus 14.

Roasted egg. The egg can represent the destruction of the Temple and/or the symbol of new life. It can also represent the free-will offering that was given along with the lamb in subsequent Passovers.

Elijah. At the end of the Seder, the children look for Elijah by opening the door. In Jewish Seders, Elijah's cup of wine stays untouched while they wait for Elijah's return. Christians recognize that their Messiah has already come. Pour a small amount of Elijah's juice into each child's third cup, and everyone can share in drinking Elijah's cup in a spirit of joy.

Questions

- The celebration of the Passover feast helps us remember when God set the Jews free. How do you think the Jewish people felt when they were finally on their way to the promised land?
- Jesus sets us free from the penalty of our sins and makes a way for us to be on our way to heaven. How is this like the way God set the Jews free?
- What can you do to help remember all Jesus did for you?

Story Extension Activities

- To celebrate our Christian Passover, have the children each paint one side of five wide craft sticks red. They arrange them into the shape of a doorway. Then they rearrange the craft sticks into the shape of a cross. On the back of the sticks, let the kids write, "Without the shedding of blood, there is no forgiveness [of sins]. Hebrews 9:22." Let them use these sticks as a tool for sharing their faith.
- Jesus was sacrificed for the sins of the world at the very hour the Passover lamb was slain. Have the children read the following verses and write down on paper how Jesus is the Lamb of God: Isaiah 53:7-9; Matthew 27:12-14; John 1:29; 1 Peter 1:19; and Revelation 5:12. Lay the papers on the tray that the lamb shank was served on.

Other Story Possibilities

You can use food to tell many tasty tales. Touching a taste bud makes sense!

- Tell the story of the manna and quail using a roasted chicken as the quail. Have the children smash white bread with a rolling pin and then use a cookie cutter or round lid to cut out circles of bread. While the children hide their eyes, scatter the "manna" all over the table, in cups, on chairs and everywhere to make it look like the manna rained down from heaven. See Exodus 16.
- This idea edibly illustrates the story of the Jews wandering in the wilderness (Numbers 14:26-35 and portions of Joshua). Pour a package of yellow cake mix into a large resealable plastic bag. The children can trace their fingers through it to represent the forty years of rambling about in the desert. Have cupcakes prepared from same type of mix ready for the children. Have them dip the cupcakes in honey, and serve with milk and joy to celebrate the Jews finally entering the land flowing with milk and honey.

4-5

Picture This

Divide your group into teams, and have them visualize, interpret, and act out each of the Ten Commandments. Designate a photographer or team of photographers to capture the essence of each of the commandments on print film, and create a display of the photographs. Let the class guess what picture is which commandment. Kids will enjoy this challenging assignment—to illustrate the invisible.

The Story

Ten Commandments, Exodus 20

The Point

God gives special rules.

The Materials

An instant-print camera with flash and at least twelve sheets of film, poster board, masking tape, and a collection of props to illustrate the Ten Commandments. (See below.) A 35-mm camera with 200 ISO film and a flash will also do, but the effects won't be as immediate. A disposable camera with a flash is also fine.

Preparation

Gather the supplies. This project may require two class periods to give the film a chance to get developed. You may want to turn it into a three-day project to give the kids time to plan their pictures and bring props from home if necessary.

Directions

Form teams. While you read the story, point to a team. They will run to the center of the room and select props from the pile on the floor. Then they will strike a pose while you snap their picture. Continue with the story, and let the next team strike a pose. You can use the suggestions given or come up with your own ideas. Give the kids plenty of time to figure out their own picture before giving them help. When the film is developed, have the kids tape the photographs to the poster board. The class then guesses which picture represents which commandment and labels each picture.

Let's Begin

Moses had led the Israelites out of Egypt, through the Red Sea, and into the desert. God fed them and protected them. God said, "See how I have taken care of you and carried you on eagles' wings. If you obey my commands, then out of all the nations, you will be my treasured possession. Although the whole earth is mine, you will be my special family."

"We will do everything the Lord has said," the people replied. Moses told the people to show they were serious by washing their clothes. *(Snap a picture of some kids scrubbing clothes with water and soap.)*

God called Moses up to the top of Mount Sinai. Thunder crashed, lightning flashed, and a thick cloud covered the mountain. The whole mountain was covered with smoke and trembled violently. The people shook with fear too. Moses was wrapped in a cloud, the glory of God. *(Photograph a child standing behind a cloud made from poster board or synthetic fiber.)*

God gave Moses many commands on how the people should treat each other and worship him. God himself wrote ten special rules on two stone tablets for his special family. They are called the Ten Commandments.

1. You shall have no other gods before me. *(Snap a close-up picture of a child in prayer.)*

2. You shall not make for yourself an idol. *(A child bows to toy cars, money, magazines with celebrities' pictures on the covers, fake jewelry, a diploma, and a football helmet or maybe some video games.)*

3. You shall not misuse the name of the Lord your God. *(Look in some cartoon strips to see the symbols used to denote swearing. Write them down on a big piece of poster board, and cut it out to look like a cartoon bubble. Let one child hold it as though the words are coming out of the opened mouth of another child.)*

4. Remember the Sabbath day by keeping it holy. *(One child holds a hymnal, another a Bible.)*

5. Honor your father and your mother. *(Take a picture of a child obeying his mother or father, perhaps hanging up a coat.)*

6. You shall not murder. *(Photograph a child lying on the ground with a toy sword or gun nearby.)*

7. You shall not commit adultery. *(Let two kids pose as bride and groom. Use wedding rings and/or perhaps a wedding album.)*

8. You shall not steal. *(Stage a robbery, and have the offender looking over her shoulder, looking guilty while stealing something from another.)*

9. You shall not lie. *(Have a culprit at the scene of a crime with a surprised expression on his face. His elbows are in and palms turned upward as if to say, "I don't know who did this!" The scene could be a broken toy.)*

10. You shall not covet. *(Gather a pile of things kids covet into a pile, such as video games, shoes, CDs, and so on. Pose hands reaching for it.)*

God's commands were given to us as well as to the Israelites. We also are his special people.

Questions

- How do you feel when people give you rules to follow?
- Why did God give us these rules?
- Which is the hardest command for you to obey?
- How can Christ help us follow the commandments?

Story Extension Ideas

- Make realistic stone tablets using plaster from a paint department or craft store. Use aluminum foil to mold the shape of a rounded tablet. Follow the directions of the plaster by adding water, stirring, and letting it set. Put a paper clip in the back to hang. When hardened, remove tablet from the aluminum mold, and have the kids scribble on it with pencil. Use a paper towel to rub the lead around, giving it a gray color. Seal with a spray sealant. Repeat for the other side of the tablet. Write the commandments in permanent marker, and hang the tablet on the wall.
- Have the kids learn the following poem and finger motions. Then invite a class of first graders in, and let the older kids teach the poem to them.

---

1. God is one and there is no other. . . . .*(Point one finger up.)*
   He is the Lord: there is not another. . . . . .*(Raise hand up.)*
2. An idol makes God number 2. . . . .*(Hold up one finger on each hand.)*
   And second place for God won't do. . . . . .*(Cross fingers.)*
3. Three fingers keep our words in check. . . .*(Hold up three fingers.)*
   Speak God's name with respect. . . . .*(Cover and uncover mouth with three fingers.)*
4. Four fingers stand for arms and feet. . . . . .*(Hold up four fingers.)*
   Remember the Sabbath day to keep. . . . . .*(Walk four fingers on your arm.)*
5. God gives us parents when we're small. . . .*(Turn palm down toward floor.)*
   Honor them while you grow tall. . . . .*(Raise it higher.)*
6. Five fingers for a body . . . .*(Hold up five fingers on one hand)*
   One finger for a sword. . . . .*(and one finger on the other hand.)*
   Do not kill another . . . .*(One finger stabs into the other five.)*
   Is the commandment of the Lord.
7. God made a husband and a wife . . . .*(Hold up two fingers on one hand, five on the other.)*
   To stay together all through life. . . . .*(Lay down two fingers, facing up; five represent blanket covering them.)*
8. Ten take away two is eight. . . . .*(Hold up ten fingers. Then put two fingers down.)*
   Stealing is a sin God hates.

9. You aren't 10; you're number 9 . . . . *(Hold up ten fingers; then put one finger down.)*

   Speak the truth: you'll do just fine.

10. Ten fingers pulling in, in, in. . . . . *(Turn palms up, pulling in.)*

    To want, want, want can be a sin.

These hand motions were adapted from Evangelizing Today's Child, July/August 1995.

Other Story Possibilities

Almost any Bible story can be acted out and recorded on film.

● Jesus casting out a demon would make for some dramatic scenes. There are many accounts to select from: Matthew 17:14-18, Mark 5, and Luke 4:33-37. For foam coming out of the mouth, whip cream in a blender until it looks like suds.

● Animate the story of Solomon's wise judgement of the babies. You'll need a baby doll and a play sword. See 1 Kings 3:16-28.

4-5

To Tell the Truth

This Biblical rendition of "To Tell the Truth" has three different versions of the Bible story. Only one is the true Biblical narrative. The class listens and then probes the Word of God for the truth. To make this even more fun, we tell the story of Balaam's talking donkey from the animal's point of view. Will the real donkey please giddy up?

The Story

Balaam's Donkey, Numbers 22:21-41

The Point

We can trust God even when we can't understand.

The Materials

For each child: photocopies of the handout titled "Donkey Tales" (pp. 44-45), paper, pencil, and a Bible

Preparation

Ask three adult volunteers to read one of the versions below for your class. Ask them to use a silly donkey's voice. Give each volunteer a copy of his or her script.

Directions

Have copies of the three tales ready to give to children after the presentations. They can try to figure out which is the honest donkey by going to their Bibles and comparing the real story with the copies of the three stories. Remember that the goal is to have children dive into Scripture to discover the truth. The correct version here is the last one. Read the correct version last of all so the truth will ring in their ears.

Let's Begin

See the handout on pages 44-45.

DONKEY TALES

Donkey's Tale #1

My name is Dudley, Dudley Donkey, and do I have a tale for you. I mean, I have my own tail, but this tale is a story. My owner's name is Balaam. He is a funny sort of guy. God has given him special power. He blesses people and curses them. Probably depends on how much money they give him. One day some fancy princes came to our house. They were messengers from the king of Moab. They said, "The king is afraid of the Israelites. Put a curse on the Israelites for him." They offered him lots of money.

But God said to Balaam, "Do not go. You must not curse Israel, because the people are blessed."

So Balaam said, "Even if the king gave me his palace filled with silver and gold, I can still only say what the Lord my God commands me to say."

Balaam saddled me up, and off we trotted. All of a sudden, he yelled, "Turn back! I see an angel of the Lord standing in the road with his sword!" I couldn't see anything, so I kept on trotting along. Next thing I knew, I was getting beaten by Balaam. Whack, whack on the side. Ouch! Hey, I didn't do anything! But I plodded along between a narrow path with walls on both sides.

Balaam yelled again, "Turn back, you stubborn donkey. I don't want to get sliced in two!" I just figured he must be crazy and kept trotting along. He beat me again with his staff. It was too much.

I said to him—hey, donkeys aren't supposed to talk, but I did. I opened my mouth, and out came real words—not a hee or a haw, but real words. You know—Hebrew words. I said, "Why are you beating me?"

Balaam answered, "You've made a fool of me. If I had a sword in my hand, I would kill you right now."

"I'm your trustworthy donkey. Have I been in the habit of doing this to you?"

"No," he said. Then I saw the angel of the Lord standing in the road with his sword drawn. Gulp. My master had saved my life.

"I'm sorry, I've behaved like such a...well...such a donkey," I said.

We went on our way and Balaam obeyed God. He blessed Israel just as God had told him to do. And then he climbed on my back, and we trotted home.

Donkey's Tale #2

My name is Dudley, Dudley Donkey, and do I have a tale for you. I mean, I have my own tail, but this tale is a story. My owner's name is Balaam. He is a funny sort of guy. God has given him special power. He blesses people and curses them. Probably depends on how much money they give him. One day some fancy princes came to our house. They were messengers from the king of Moab. They said, "The king wants you to bless the Israelites. He knows that God is on their side. He hopes if you bless them, then they won't harm his country." They offered Balaam lots of money.

God said to Balaam, "Go on and bless my people."

So Balaam said, "Okay." He saddled me up, and off we trotted. All of a sudden, I saw an angel of the Lord standing in the road with his sword. Whoa. I wasn't about to mess with that angel, so I turned off the road into a field. Next thing I knew, I'm getting beaten by Balaam. Whack, whack on the side. Ouch! Hey, I didn't do anything! But I plodded along between a narrow path with walls on both sides. Whoa. There was that angel again with its sword flashing in the afternoon sun. I pressed close to the wall so the angel wouldn't slice my master Balaam in half. And what do I get? Beaten again.

The angel appeared again. I did the only thing I could. I lay right down. Well, that drove my master crazy. He picked up his staff and started beating me again, real hard. It was too much. I said to him—hey, donkeys aren't supposed to talk, but I did. I opened my mouth, and out came real words—not a hee or a haw, but real words. You know—Hebrew words. I said, "What have I done that you've beaten me three times?"

Balaam answered, "You've made a fool of me. If I had a sword in my hand, I would kill you right now."

"I'm your trustworthy donkey. Have I been in the habit of doing this to you?"

"No," he said. Then the Lord opened Balaam's eyes, and he saw the angel of the Lord standing in the road with his sword drawn. He realized that I had saved his life. Hee-haw. It made him look a bit like...you know...a donkey. He fell face down and said, "I have sinned."

We went on our way, and Balaam obeyed God. He blessed Israel, just as God had told him to do. And then he climbed on my back, and we trotted home.

Donkey's Tale #3

My name is Dudley, Dudley Donkey, and do I have a tale for you. I mean, I have my own tail, but this tale is a story. My owner's name is Balaam. He is a funny sort of guy. God has given him special power. He blesses people and curses them. Probably depends on how much money they give him. One day some fancy princes came to our house. They were messengers from the king of Moab. They said, "The king is afraid of the Israelites. Put a curse on the Israelites for him." They offered him lots of money.

But God said to Balaam, "Do not go. You must not curse Israel, because the people are blessed."

So Balaam said, "Even if the king gave me his palace filled with silver and gold, I can still only say what the Lord my God commands me to say."

Balaam saddled me up, and off we trotted. All of a sudden, I saw an angel of the Lord standing in the road with his sword. Whoa. I wasn't about to mess with that angel, so I turned off the road into a field. Next thing I knew, I'm getting beaten by Balaam. Whack, whack. He hits me on the side. Ouch. Hey, I didn't do anything! But I plodded along a narrow path with walls on both sides. Whoa, there was that angel again with its sword flashing in the afternoon sun. I pressed close to the wall so the angel wouldn't slice my master Balaam in half. And what do I get? Beaten again.

The angel appeared again. I did the only thing I could. I lay right down. Well, that drove my master crazy. He picked up his staff and started beating me again, real hard. It was too much. I said to him—hey, donkeys aren't supposed to talk, but I did. I opened my mouth, and out came real words—not a hee or a haw, but real words. You know—Hebrew words. I said, "What have I done that you've beaten me three times?"

Balaam answered me, "You've made a fool of me. If I had a sword in my hand, I would kill you right now."

"I'm your trustworthy donkey. Have I been in the habit of doing this to you?"

"No," he said. Then the Lord opened Balaam's eyes, and he saw the angel of the Lord standing in the road with his sword drawn. He realized that I had saved his life. Hee-haw. It made him look a bit like...you know...a donkey. He fell face down and said, "I have sinned."

We went on our way, and Balaam obeyed God. He blessed Israel just as God had told him to do. And then he climbed on my back, and we trotted home.

Questions

- How did Balaam feel when he didn't understand the donkey's actions?
- Tell about a time when you didn't understand why something was happening.
- How will you respond to God when you can't understand what is happening around you?

Story Extension Ideas

- Help your kids to see God's unseen sovereign hand. Have the kids interview adults in their lives with the following questions: Can you think of a time when God saved you from disaster, but you didn't know it until later? How did you feel at the time? How do you feel about it now? Vote for the story that best illustrates the concept that God can see what is best for us when we can't.
- Read Numbers 22:32: "I have come to oppose you because your path is a reckless one before me." Use chairs to set up a narrow aisle, and let students each squeeze between the chairs while reading a prayer they wrote, asking God to keep them safe from reckless behavior as they grow.

Other Story Possibilities

- Almost any Bible story can be told in a "to-tell-the-truth" game. Choose short versions. Let the class write their own versions. Secretly select two of the children to distort their version. The story of Paul's arrival on Malta in Acts 28 has many facets. You can tell one version where he encourages the natives to worship him, one where he dies of the snakebite, and the real version.
- Tell three tales of Peter's denial of Christ. The first rendition could have Peter hanging himself as Judas did from the guilt of the denial. In the second version, he can admit to being a follower of Jesus Christ. The third is sadly the truth: He does deny Christ. See Mark 14:66-72 and Luke 22:54-62.

K-1

You Are There

The Word of God is living and active like...children! Why should we make God's word static when it sizzles with energy and emotion? This storytelling technique shows how to make these five chapters of Joshua come to life. Together the class will join Joshua as they hide under "flax," pile up rocks, cross the Jordan, and blast Jericho to pieces.

The Story

Jericho, Joshua 2–6

The Point

The battle is the Lord's.

The Materials

Newspaper, scarlet ribbon, milk, cups, graham crackers, honey, plastic knife, at least ten sheets of blue 8½x11 paper, blocks for Jericho, and enough rocks and paper towel tubes for each child. Optional: toy sword, rope.

Preparation

If you don't have enough paper towel tubes for horns for each child, cut them in half. If you don't have blocks to use to build Jericho, you can collect cereal boxes to use. Push the chairs back, and place a table in the middle of the room. Set out a Jordan River. Lay out the construction paper in a row. Hide rocks beneath the middle of the river. If you don't have a carpeted area for the kids to sit on, bring in some blankets.

Directions

Involve as many children as possible in all the parts of this story. Gather the children together on the carpeted area to begin.

Let's Begin

After Moses died, Joshua became the new leader of the Israelites. The Israelites, also known as the Jews, were God's people. It was Joshua's job to bring the Israelites into the land God had promised, a land flowing with milk and honey. That means the land was rich with green pastures, cattle were scattered on the hills, and the fields were full of flowers with bees buzzing all about.

The Israelites had lived in the hot desert

for forty years. They couldn't wait to eat some juicy grapes and sip some creamy milk. And they wanted a home. They wanted to enjoy the shade of the palm trees and smell the luscious roses. They were so tired of living in tents and wandering around in the desert. Their first stop would be the city of Jericho.

But there was a problem—a big problem. Big people lived behind the big walls in the big cities and did not want to give up their towns for the Israelites.

(Have the children build the blocks on a table to represent the walls of Jericho. Then have them sit back down.)

The Lord said, "It is time for the Israelites to cross the Jordan River into the land I am about to give to them. I am the God who loves you. I will never leave you. Be strong and brave. Read my words and remember them. Do not be terrified, for I, the Lord your God, will be with you wherever you go."

And the people said, *(Have the children repeat this after you.)* "Whatever you tell us, we will do. And wherever you send us, we will go. We will obey the Lord."

(Pick a child to be Joshua.) So Joshua sent two men as spies into the city of Jericho to check it out. *(Have Joshua pick two children.)* They sneaked into the city past the huge gates *(Use two chairs as the city gates.)* and walls that were twenty feet thick and twenty-five feet high. *(Show the children how big that is. Have the children tiptoe around Jericho with their eyes shaded, peeking about, and then sit back down.)* They found a room to stay in, the home of a woman named Rahab. Now there is a reason that, after more than three thousand years, we know Rahab's name. She became a special friend to the men and a friend of God. *(Choose a child to be Rahab.)*

Someone told the king of Jericho, "Israelites are here to spy out our land."

But Rahab knew that the two Israelites were on God's side and that God was on the Israelites' side. So she whispered to the men, "Follow me." They quietly climbed up to the top of the roof. By the light of the moon, Rahab hid the men under some flax, which is like wheat. *(Have the two spies lie down, and have Rahab spread newspaper over them. Turn out the lights.)* While they men were lying there, completely quiet and trying not to move or sneeze, they heard the soldiers' footsteps *(Make the sound of footsteps.)* marching past them. The spies prayed silently that the king's soldiers wouldn't hear their hearts pounding from fear. Perhaps they heard the soldiers stop right in front of them.

(In a deep voice) Where are the men? We know you let them stay here! Don't you know they are our enemies?

Rahab said, "Yes, the men came to me, but I did not know they were Israelites. They left just before the gates were shut for the night. Go after them quickly. You may catch up with them." So the king's soldiers raced out the gates after the men. Rahab took the flax off the spies. She whispered, "I know the Lord has given this land to you. Everyone in Jericho is terrified of you Israelites. All of us living inside these great walls of Jericho are melting with fear. When we heard that your God is mighty and fights for you, our hearts sank. Your Lord is God in heaven above and on the earth below. Please promise that you won't harm me or my family when you destroy this city."

And the men said, "Our lives for your lives! We will protect you." *(Have the children repeat this.)* They told her to tie this red ribbon in her window. They told her that when they destroyed the city, they would not harm her or her family inside. *(Have one child hang the scarlet ribbon from the wall of Jericho.)*

Rahab's house was on top of the wall, so she let the spies climb down a rope hanging out a window. *(Have the children take turns holding onto the rope and backing across the room while you hold the rope taut.)* And so the spies escaped from Jericho. They hid in the hills and then went back to camp.

Joshua said, "What did you find out, spies?" *(Joshua repeats. Let the children share their adventure.)* Joshua said, "The Lord has surely given the whole land into our hands; all the people are melting in fear. Get ready, for the Lord will do amazing things among you. This is how you will know that the living God is among you." So the people got ready.

(Stand on one side of the Jordan River.) The river was at flood stage and could have been a mile wide. How would you get a million people across a river? *(Pause for children to give possible solutions.)*

There were no boats or bridges. They couldn't swim across with all their belongings and children. So God did a miracle. Just as soon as the priests set foot in the Jordan River, the water stopped flowing. It just stopped. The people looked and where the river had been was now dry ground! The people marched themselves right across the sandy spot that had been the Jordan River just minutes before. *(Part the water, revealing the rocks, and have the children walk through. On their way, they each pick up a rock from the dry ground.)* They stacked up the rocks in a pile to remember the miracle that God had done for them. *(Have the children make a stack from the rocks they picked up.)* Behind them they heard a mighty roaring sound and spun around. They turned just in time to see the river splashing and frothing, racing back to its river banks. The dry ground was gone. The deep Jordan River was back to normal.

(Select a child to hold the sword.) Joshua looked up and saw a man standing in front of him with a sword in his hand. *(Have your Joshua act this out.)* Joshua bowed down to this angel from the Lord. The angel told Joshua, "I have given Jericho into your hands. March around the city six times, once each day, blowing on your trumpets. On the seventh day, march around the city seven times, and then give a mighty shout. The walls of the city will collapse."

(Distribute "horns," and have the children follow you, buzzing on their horns and counting as you go around the block city. After the seventh rotation, stop.) Shout! For the Lord has given you the city! But save Rahab and her family. Her house is the one with the red ribbon. *(Let the kids shout and knock down the walls.)* And so they took the city. The Lord was with Joshua and the Israelites. They were in their land flowing with milk and honey. *(Serve the kids graham crackers with honey and milk.)*

Questions

- How do you think the Iraelites felt when they walked aound the city with only trumpets?
- How do you feel when there is a big problem in your life?
- How is this big problem like the big walls of Jericho?
- How can you let God fight for you when you have a big problem?

Story Extension Ideas

- For a simple craft, fold a piece of blue paper into thirds so that the sides open up. This will represent the Jordan River. On the middle section, the children can draw fish and glue down sand and small seashells. On the outside, they can copy this poem:

  We crossed the river on dry ground
  And watched the walls come tumbling down.
  Our God is big and great and strong.
  I will praise him all day long.

- Children are never too young to learn that there is a "crimson thread" (the idea of redemption by blood) woven throughout Scripture. Use putty to attach a scarlet ribbon to the top of a wall. Place pictures behind it from old Sunday school material. Include pictures from other Bible stories where blood has been a means of salvation, such as the Passover and Jesus on the cross.

Other Story Possibilities

Note from the story above how the children are included at every opportunity, using repetition, questions, motion, and simulation. Try to pick out the ways that the story has been acted out. Ask God to give you wisdom as you bring your own Bible stories to life.

- The story of Hagar and Ishmael found in Genesis 21 can be easily acted out. Have the kids munch on crackers to experience thirst in the desert. They can wander around as though lost and be revived with water. Make your own well out of a box and a bucket or pail, and use a ladle to scoop out the water.
- Children can become the disciples at the Last Supper, complete with foot washing and Judas slipping out to betray Christ. Use juice for the wine and flattened white bread for the unleavened bread. See Matthew 26:17-30, Luke 22:7-23, and John 13:1-30.

2-5

Shadow Dancing

Children of all ages and any size audience love to watch a shadow show. The play is acted out behind a white sheet, while a light from behind the actors casts silhouettes onto the sheet. In this story, mighty Samson becomes a mere shadow of his formerly strong self.

The Story

Samson and Delilah, Judges 13–16

The Point

Put God before our own desires.

The Materials

Poster board, yarn, Biblical outfits for each actor or actress, white sheet to be secured to the ceiling, items to secure sheet (tacks or small nails), a lamp or overhead projector, newspaper, scissors, rags, wine glass with water, pennies, and a baby doll

Preparation

Ask several high school kids to act out this play for children in grades two through five. Prepare the props by having the high schoolers cut out pillars, a large circle for a grindstone, flames, large scissors, and a jawbone out of poster board and cut strips of newspaper for the wheat bundle. Fashion a yarn wig for Samson. Stuff his shirt with rags to create large muscles. To set up the stage, hang the sheet from the ceiling with tacks or small nails. Place the light source behind it, leaving plenty of room between the sheet and the light for the action of the play. Have the actors think visually as though they were in the audience. Profiles work best. The actors can combine roles if they'd like. Have them exaggerate their motions and listen carefully to the script so they can follow the prompts in bold.

Directions

Practice until the show is smooth. The reader should read clearly and slowly, emphasizing the actions in bold print. If you are using a spotlight, be careful so robes don't get caught.

Let's Begin

A woman was out in the field one day, bundling sheaves of wheat. ***(Have someone hold strips of newspaper for the woman to collect.)*** As she went about her work, she dreamed of having her own little bundle of joy—a baby. ***(Cradles bundle and rocks it.)*** Then she **sat down** and cried, for she knew she would never be able to have a baby.

But an **angel of the Lord appeared** to her and said, "God can do anything. You are going to have a son!" The woman was so happy. ***(Woman throws arms up.)***

The **woman ran** to tell her husband, **Manoah**, the good news. **Manoah hugged his wife** and praised the Lord ***(hands up in the air).*** Then Manoah **got down on his knees and prayed**: "O Lord, I beg you, let the man of God return to teach us how to raise the boy who is to be born."

God heard Manoah. The **angel came back** and said, "The boy should never drink wine, and his hair should never be cut. He is special to God."

The woman gave birth to a boy and named him Samson. ***(Woman holds a baby doll.)*** He grew ***(Woman puts baby doll down; Samson enters.)*** and the Lord blessed him. The Holy Spirit of God began to stir in him. But he had a little problem. Whatever Samson wanted, Samson got. ***(Samson shakes fists and puts hands on hips.)***

One day when he was grown, he said to his parents, "I saw a Philistine girl ***(Points.)*** and was she pretty! ***(Shakes hand.)*** I want her. ***(Shakes fists up and down.)*** Now get her for me." He said it just like that.

His father and mother replied ***(shaking finger)***, "Samson, must you marry a Philistine? They are our enemies. They don't even worship the true God. They worship idols."

"I want her," Samson said, **stomping his foot**. "Get her for me!"

And so, whatever Samson wanted, Samson got. He had strong muscles and a strong will. ***(Flexes muscles.)*** Samson and his parents were **walking** to the girl's city when suddenly a lion came roaring out of the woods. The Spirit of the Lord came upon Samson so that he tore the lion apart with his bare hands! ***(Rips a piece of paper.)*** That's how strong he was. ***(Flexes muscles.)*** But unfortunately, he didn't use his strength for God's good plans—he used it to get revenge.

Samson had one weakness, and that was for beautiful women. He fell in love with a woman named Delilah. The **Philistines sneaked up to Delilah and whispered** to her, "See if you can get Samson to tell you the secret of his great strength so we can capture him. We'll give you eleven hundred shekels of silver." ***(Drops some pennies into Delilah's hands.)***

So Delilah ***(Puts hand on Samson.)*** said to Samson, "Tell me the secret of your great strength."

Samson lied to her. He said, "If you tie me up with seven fresh strings from a bow and arrow, I'll become as weak as any other man."

So the Philistines **brought her seven fresh bowstrings**. While **Samson was sleeping, Delilah tied him up. With the men hidden, she called to him,** "Samson, the

Philistines are upon you!" Samson **snapped the strings** as if they were nothing.

Delilah **stamped her foot** and pouted. She said, "You made a fool out of me. You lied to me!" Then **she put her head on his shoulder** and, in her soft voice, said, "Come on, tell me how you can be tied up."

Samson said, "If anyone ties me with new ropes that have never been used, I'll become as weak as any other man."

So Delilah **took new ropes and tied him with them. With the Philistines hidden** in the room, **she called** to him, "Samson, the Philistines are upon you!"

He **hopped up and snapped** off the rope as though it were nothing, laughing.

Delilah **stomped her foot** and cried, "How can you say 'I love you' when you won't tell me the secret of your great strength?" Delilah nagged him every day until he was sick to death of it.

Finally he said, "All right, my hair has never been cut. If my hair were cut, my strength would leave me. I'd become as weak as any other man."

When **he fell asleep, Delilah called the Philistines.** and they cut off his seven long locks of hair. ***(Use the clipping shears to cut off the hair made of yarn.)*** As his **hair fell** to the ground, his strength really did leave him. You see, the Lord had left him.

This time when Delilah called, "Samson, the Philistines are upon you," **he jumped** up. The **Philistines grabbed him.** He had no strength to fight them. They gouged out his eyes and put chains on him. ***(Rattle chains or car keys.)*** Then Samson had to **push a huge stone** around and around every day to grind grain. Blind and **stumbling**, with the shackles cutting into his feet, ***(Rattle chains.)*** Samson had a lot of time to think. He thought about how he had messed up his life. He prayed to God to forgive him. As he spent day after day **pushing** the grinding stone in prison, his faith grew. Something else was growing too—his hair. But the Philistines didn't notice.

One day the Philistines held a huge celebration to honor Dagon. Dagon was their fake god who was half fish, half man. Stuffing their mouths with food and their bellies with wine, ***(Hold up a wineglass and let the water slosh out.)*** they called for Samson to come from prison. He staggered about in his darkness. People shrieked with laughter, **pushing Samson around and hitting him. They teased him with food only to toss it at him.** When they were through, **a servant led Samson away.** Samson said, "Put me where I can feel the pillars so I can lean against them." Those two pillars held up the entire building that held the party of three thousand men and women.

Samson prayed to the Lord, "O God, please strengthen me one more time." Then **Samson stood between the two pillars and began to push.** He prayed, "Let me die with the Philistines." He took a great breath and pushed again. Creeaaaaakkk. One of the **huge stone pillars began to move.**

Somebody yelled, "Look at Samson!" Samson took another breath. With **shaking arms, he pushed** until it hurt. A **pillar moved** a few more inches. The music stopped. The laughing stopped. Everyone stood frozen as though they were watching a dream. Samson gathered all his might and **pushed again** with all the power he could. Creeeaaakkkkk. Gggrrrrr. This time **the pillars toppled over.**

The people started to scream and run, but it was too late. The roof of the temple came crashing down, crushing every Philistine in the place. Of course, Samson died too. He killed many more when he died than while he lived. What a life his could have been!

Questions

- Samson could have been a mighty man of God. Why did Samson turn away from obeying God?
- How do you feel when your parents or teachers say "no" to you?
- How are we sometimes like Samson?
- How can you put God ahead of your own desires?

Story Extension Ideas

- Play a game called Backward Choices. Have the children line up facing the wall with their Bibles in hand, opened to Judges 14. Mark out a finish line somewhere across the room. The kids search their Bibles to find the wrong choices Samson made. For each wrong choice they find, they can take a step backward. Continue until someone reaches the finish line.
- Read the script aloud, and let the kids stand up and act out the motions with you.

Other Story Possibilities

For other shadow shows, look for stories that have a lot of action and just a few characters. Let the class work together to write the story. They'll learn to search the Scriptures for keys to express feeling, motions, and words to make stories come to life.

- Jesus clearing the Temple is full of action and feeling. Have the kids look up and compare versions in Luke 19:45-48, John 2:12-25, and Matthew 21:12-14.
- The story of Peter walking on the water is well suited to this type of presentation also. See Matthew 14:22-33.

K-1

Indoor Camp Out

Show me a child who doesn't love a bedtime story. You'll never have to say, "Sit up and listen" while they camp out indoors! Lay blankets and pillows on the carpet for a peaceful time to ponder the Psalms. Glow-in-the-dark stars add a touch of reality as you read to the children about David, the shepherd-psalmist. The story of David's anointing is interwoven with the Psalms. Soft music in the background will lend an aura of wonder to the words, "O, Lord our Lord, how majestic is your name in all the earth!

The Story

A Psalmist's Story, 1 Samuel 16; Psalms 8, 19, 23

The Point

God cares about our feelings.

The Materials

Glow-in-the-dark stars; putty; tape recorder; soft music on tape; small flashlight covered with red cellophane; blankets; pillows; pieces of cardboard; if possible, a small guitar or lyre

Preparation

The week before, ask the children to bring their own pillows to class. Put the stars on the ceiling or a wall using removable putty. Prepare the stars under fluorescent lights as they work the best in getting the stars to glow. The more stars you use, the more impressive the effect will be. If you don't have many stars, concentrate them into one area. Make sure the room can be completely darkened. Cover the flashlight with red cellophane so you can read the script without ruining the effect of the stars. Lay out all the blankets. Plug in your tape recorder, and have the tape ready to go.

Directions

Have the kids lie down, and get a helper to help you with the special effects. Turn out the lights in the room once the kids are settled.

Let's Begin

"David, get out there, and take the sheep to the west pasture to graze," Abinadab said. He was one of David's older brothers.

"It's your turn today," David replied.

Abinadab stood up, towering over David. He grabbed David by his cloak and hissed, "Do it, or I'll tell Dad that you let Miss Misty wander off into the thicket while you were playing your stupid harp."

"Oh, all right," David grumbled. "Besides, Miss Misty is the rottenest sheep we have. Why did I have to get stuck being the littlest brother?"

Gathering his harp, sling, and some food in a sack, David headed out for the pasture. He didn't really mind. It was a sunny day, and there was a poem he was in the middle of writing. David hiked over the rocky fields and opened the gate. He was surrounded instantly by white, woolly baaaas and black, wet muzzles tickling him. David laughed and opened the gate to the west pasture. With a little tap of his rod here and a gentle shove with his staff there, David led the sheep to fresh fields of green grass.

"Ah, my favorite hideaway," David said, as he settled himself against a huge oak tree. Water danced over the rocks in the stream beside him, making splashing and gurgling sounds. He took a deep breath. A warm summer breeze sent the sweet smell of clover into his being. Sunshine soaked through David's skin into his very soul, warming his heart.

(Have a helper turn on the music, turn on a faucet, or pour water slowly into a basin and wave a piece of cardboard at the kids to simulate a warm breeze.)

Strumming his lyre, *(If available, strum on guitar or lyre.)* David sang, "I am like a sheep. The Lord is my shepherd; I have everything that I need. He makes me lie down in green pastures, he leads me beside quiet waters, he restores my soul. He guides me in paths that are right for his name's sake. Even though I walk through the valley of death, I will fear no evil, for you are with me. Your rod and your staff, they comfort me." *(Stop music, water, and fan.)*

David had no idea that back at his home, something amazing was happening. Samuel was at his own house! Samuel was a judge, prophet, and God's chosen priest—a very important man. Samuel had come to pick out a new king of Israel.

No one bothered to find David and tell him. Samuel, the priest, said to David's father, Jesse, "I have come to tell you whom the Lord has chosen as the new king." Eliab, the oldest son, stood up and strutted over to Samuel. Samuel looked up into Eliab's proud, brown eyes and thought, "Surely, this must be the man." But the Lord said, "No, he will not be the king. Don't think about how tall or handsome he is. Man looks at the outside of a person. But not God. God looks at a person's heart."

Then Abinadab walked in front of Samuel thinking, It must be God's will that I wasn't out in the fields today. But he was wrong. God hadn't picked him either. All seven of David's older brothers walked past Samuel, including Shammah, Nethanel, Raddai, and Ozem. But, no, not one of them was chosen by God to be the king. Samuel asked Jesse, "Are these all the sons you have?"

"Well, there is one more, but he's too young," Jesse answered, "He is out tending the sheep."

"Go get him. We will not sit down until he

arrives," Samuel said.

By this time, it was getting dark. The stars were beginning to peek out of the heavens. David was throwing sticks onto the fire. As he watched the flames rise and fall, he gazed into the orangish-blue heat. He started to hum a tune. He liked it!

David pulled out his lyre and sang, "Lord, you prepare a table before me, even in the middle of all my enemies. You anoint my head with oil. I feel like a king! My cup of blessings overflows. Surely goodness and love will follow me all the days of my life, and I will live in the house of the Lord forever and ever and…"

Just then Abinadab came running up to him. "Hurry," he huffed, trying to catch his breath. "You need to get home right away."

"Is everything all right?" David asked.

"Oh, I'd say everything is more than all right. Just hurry."

David doused the flames, threw his lyre into his sack, and ran home, tripping over rocks in the dusk. David threw the door open and found his brothers and father all around the table with a stranger. Samuel looked at David and knew. David was sun-tanned and handsome, but Samuel saw past all that. He saw that David's heart beat for God.

"Rise and anoint him. He is the one," the Lord said.

Samuel poured the oil over David's bowed head. That was the sign that he would be king someday. His brothers watched and wondered. That day, the Spirit of the Lord came upon David in power. It was the beginning of an amazing God-led life.

After Samuel had left and David's father and brothers were all asleep, David carried his harp up onto the roof of his house. Under the stars, a warm, summer breeze calmed David's pounding heart. He looked up into the heavens and sang softly, "The heavens tell of God's glory, the stars tell his story. Your words make me wise, O Lord; you bring joy to my heart. Therefore, I will praise you. You, O Lord, keep my lamp burning; my God turns my darkness into light!" *(Turn on the light.)*

God turned David's dark days into bright ones. God loved David and David loved God. We can love God like that too, for he loves you as much as he does David.

Questions

- What are some feelings that David may have had in this story?
- What feelings have you had that are like David's?
- David sang and later wrote down his feelings. How can you tell God your feelings?

Story Extension Ideas

- Make a lyre for each child in your class. A lyre is made of two pieces of flat wood fastened at right angles. Strings are stretched across the frame so that the lyre takes the shape of a triangle. The kids themselves can pound tacks into the wood and stretch rubber bands from tack to tack. Let them strum their lyres to the psalms.

● Talk about loving people for who they are rather than for their outer appearances. Teach the kids this poem:

Saul was tall, but his heart was small.
Saul looked strong, but he acted wrong.
Even a king can be a fool
If he won't obey God's rules.

Other Story Possibilities

● Tell the story of God's promise to Abraham to make his family as numerous as the stars in the sky. See Genesis 15.

● Under the witness of the stars, David spared Saul's life. Share the story of David sneaking up on King Saul while he slept in 1 Samuel 26.

K-3

Setting in the Scene

Recreating a setting can have a powerful impact on the listeners. Why not use nature as your classroom? Imagine bringing a group of children into a cave and telling them the story of David sparing King Saul's life. This particular story is told in second person, present tense to further impress the reality of the story upon the listeners.

The Story

David Spares Saul, 1 Samuel 24:1-22

The Point

We can share God's mercy.

The Materials

Large chairs, a flashlight, a tarp, a piece of purple cloth, several large rocks, and (for each child) a water bottle, a plastic bag with a few crackers, and a small piece of fabric

Preparation

You can turn your classroom into a cave by turning tables and lining up chairs to create the skeleton of the cave. The tarp can be draped over it. You can also make a "cave" by running two clotheslines from tree to tree outdoors and draping dark-colored sheets and blankets over them. Use clothespins to hold the sheets or blankets in place. A tent could be set up as a substitute cave. Add large rocks here and there, inside and out, to make it more "cave-like."

Directions

Use your flashlight to read the story to the children. Follow with the questions.

Let's Begin

(Have the children sit outside the "cave.") Where can you hide six hundred men? That's what David needs to know. He and his band of six hundred men are on the run from the king. King Saul is wild with jealousy. He hates David and wants him dead! And whatever King Saul wants, King Saul gets. Most people won't say it aloud, but they think that King Saul is crazy. He has his entire army searching for David. David has been only good and honest, but now he is being hunted down like a criminal. Saul's soldiers have been searching the fields and forests.

David and his men seem to have mysteriously disappeared. You are one of them.

"I know a cave," one of the men is saying to David. "I used to hide there when I was in trouble."

"But will it hold six hundred men?" David asks.

"Oh, yes, it will hold thousands of people."

"Let's go, men," David says.

The men gather up their spears and water bottles. They wrap food in bundles of cloth. *(Have the children do this with the cloth and the bags of crackers.)* They haven't got very much. In one hand, David carries his lyre for making music. In the other hand, he carries a very heavy sword. Perhaps it had belonged to Goliath, the giant Philistine that David killed. It seemed like centuries ago. Now David carries that sword to protect his life.

Climbing higher and higher up the mountains, you start to sweat and get dizzy from the heat. The going gets tougher as you pull yourself up rocks that stick straight up. Wild goats stop to stare as if wondering, "What are you doing up here?" How you want to rest but you dare not. King Saul will surely be after your army in no time.

"We're almost there, men," David says. He is always encouraging his men. They love David and would die for him if necessary.

"Look, there's the cave!"

The men pour into the cave. *(Have the children go into the cave.)* A lot of them can be heard saying, "Oh, it feels so cool and refreshing in here." They sit down to rest and drink from their water bottles. David wisely puts a man outside the cave to keep watch for King Saul. The men are starting to get settled. As they crowd deeper into the cave to investigate, a few of them light torches. The smoke makes you cough and stings your eyes. Even with the bat guano droppings on your feet and the smell of six hundred sweaty bodies, you're still glad you aren't alone in this forsaken and lonely hide-out.

Just then you hear, "Put out your torches, quickly. Move as far back in the cave as you can. Don't move, don't cough, and don't say a word." *(Have the children squeeze into the back of the cave and sit down.)* The blood freezes in your veins. You know. King Saul's soldiers are here! And you are caught in a cave against three thousand highly trained, bloodthirsty soldiers. The men crowd toward the rear of the cave, pressing their backs against the wet, sticky walls. They squeeze together in the pitch dark. What is that touching your skin? a fellow warrior's arm or a blind tarantula? You can't even ask. You hold your breath. You want to sneeze, but you know that one sneeze or scream can mean your death. You tighten your grip on your sword.

As your eyes slowly adjust to cave darkness, you can see the silhouette of a man enter the cave. He can't see you, but you can see him. You swallow what's left of your breath. This is not just any man, not just another soldier. It's the king himself! What is he doing? Why is he by himself?

Fear grabs you. Then someone standing near David speaks your thoughts. He whispers, "David, this is your chance. The Lord said he would give your enemy into your hands, and there he is!"

David creeps up as quietly as a fox. He knows that the king can't see him. What is the king doing? He isn't! He's—what? Going to the bathroom? Even kings have to do that sometimes, and that explains why he is alone.

Your nose itches. But you don't dare sneeze. David takes out his sword. You see its sharp silhouette as he silently swings it up high. You see the sword strike. You hear a very quiet chop. You wait for the king to scream and stagger. David sneaks back to the crowd of men.

"You didn't kill him?" one of the men hisses.

"No. Look what I got." David holds up a piece of the king's robe. *(Hold up the purple cloth and pass it around.)* You touch it. David whispers, "I shouldn't have played such a rotten trick on him! After all, God has made Saul the king."

"You can still kill him," you want to yell at David. "King Saul has hunted us down like wild dogs. We've lived off berries, and our growling stomachs might betray our hiding spot." You want to raise your sword and end this nightmare. Your ears itch to hear your captain, David, say, "Go get him."

"No," David is saying. "This is not God's way. We will not attack Saul. The Lord is the stronghold of my life—revenge belongs to God."

Now you begin to wonder just who is crazy. In the darkness you shake your head, trying to understand this David. King Saul is leaving the cave. You feel anger rising through you. Just then, David stands at the mouth of the cave. He cries out, "My lord, the king!"

King Saul spins around, startled. David bow downs and lies on the ground. You hear David say, "Why do you listen when men say, 'David is bent on harming you'? See with your own eyes how the Lord gave you into my hands in the cave. Some men urged me to kill you, but I didn't. See, my father, look at this piece of your robe in my hand! I cut off the corner of your robe, but I did not kill you. Now you see that I've done nothing wrong, but you are hunting me down. Against whom has the king of Israel come out? Whom do you think you are chasing? a dead dog? a flea? May the Lord himself judge between me and you."

Your jaw drops down. Your respect for David shoots up.

Saul lifts his robe. He sees the chopped corner. He begins to shake. One minute ago, you couldn't believe your eyes. Now you can't believe your ears. The king, mighty King Saul, is crying. "David, my son. You are more righteous than I. I have treated you badly. You have treated me well. You could have killed me and you didn't! May the Lord reward you," he sobs. Now the king is on **his** knees before David. "Please, promise me that when you become king instead of me that your won't kill my family."

"I swear it by all that is holy," David says.

With that the king disappears from sight. He takes his army back home.

Your sword slips from your hand and clatters upon the rocks of the cave floor. You resist the urge to bow before David. Instead your heart bows to God. In the darkness of the cave, you begin to see a light. Words of David's songs come flooding into your brain. "Be exalted, O God, above the heavens." Oh, how very much you have to learn. All the men gather around David. But not you. Not now. With a big sigh, you wander deeper into the cave to talk with this strange God that this strange man is teaching you about. And you thank God. You pray the words your captain, David, has taught you: "Show me your ways, O Lord, teach me your paths. Guide me in your truth and teach me, for you are God, my Savior, and my hope is in you all day long."

Questions

- How do you think David's soldiers felt about Saul and his men?
- Is there someone in your life who has been unfair to you?
- How can you show mercy to this person, just as David showed mercy to Saul?
- How does God show his mercy to us?

Story Extension Ideas

- David wrote Psalm 57 when he had fled from Saul into the cave. Have the kids rewrite Psalm 57, incorporating parts of the story. For example, "I am in the midst of lions" (Three thousand of King Saul's soldiers are hunting for me, and now I am trapped in this cave.); "I lie among hungry beasts..."
- Have the children gather rocks. Let them paint the rocks and then use a permanent marker to write a verse from one of David's psalms on each rock. One good verse to choose may be "Cast your cares on the Lord and he will sustain you; he will never let the righteous fall" (Psalm 55:22).

Other Story Possibilities

Stretch your vision, and take your class into the great outdoors for more Bible story adventures.

- Daniel's fate in the lion's den would seem more real in a cave. See Daniel 6.
- Why not go to a playground that has sand to "see" Jesus write in the sand while the woman caught in adultery is threatened with her life in John 8:1-11.
- Find a grassy slope, and bring a basket of fish-shaped crackers and rolls to share with the kids while you tell the story of Jesus feeding the multitude in Matthew 14:13-21 or Mark 6:30-44.

2-5

Crowd Out Loud

These biblical readings can also be called choral readings. They can be quite beautiful, almost like a song with a spoken refrain. Reminiscent of some of the psalms, these readings involve everyone. The repetitions are echoes that will hopefully reverberate in the children's ears long after the story has ended.

The Story

Elijah on Mount Carmel, 1 Kings 18:16-39

The Point

We can depend on God.

Materials

For each child: photocopies of the handout titled "Elijah on Mount Carmel" (p. 63) and a marker

Preparation

Make photocopies of the script for each child, and assign readers. Let the kids decide what they would like to read. Some kids hate to read aloud alone but won't mind it if they can blend in with a group. Let them highlight their portions of the script. You are the leader, like the director of a symphony. Practice the script at least once so that you can get a feel for it.

Directions

Choose two strong readers for the parts of Elijah and Ahab. For more effect, you may want to be Elijah, with a helper being Ahab. Form the rest of the class into Chorus 1 and Chorus 2. You may want to do a dry run and then read it aloud together for the church or another class. Explain to the children why the word "god" is sometimes in lowercase. Be sure to help with the pronunciation of new words, such as "Carmel" and "Baal."

Let's Begin

See the handout on page 63.

ELIJAH ON MOUNT CARMEL

Ahab: Is that you, you troubler of Israel?

Elijah: I have not made trouble. You have. You have abandoned God and worshipped idols.

Ahab: I've been looking for you for three years. I've searched every kingdom, nation, and tribe for you. I've had my men look in caves and under rocks for you. You cursed the sky, and it hasn't rained for three years.

Elijah: Can I make it rain? Can I stop the rain? Who do you think I am? God?

Chorus 1: The Lord, he is God.

Elijah: We'll settle this once and for all. Go and bring your four hundred fifty prophets of your idols Baal and the four hundred prophets of the idol Asherah. Bring them and all of Israel to Mount Carmel.

Ahab: Let it be as you have said.

Elijah: Now that everyone is here, I ask, "How long will you waver between two opinions. If Baal is God, follow him. If the Lord is God, follow him.

Chorus 1: The Lord, he is God.

Elijah: I am the only prophet of the Lord left. But Baal has four hundred fifty prophets. Let's see what four hundred fifty prophets and Baal can do, shall we? We will each get a bull, cut it up, and put it on an altar of wood. Then you call on the name of your god, and I will call on the name of the Lord. The god who answers by fire—he is God.

Chorus 2: What you say is good. The god who answers by fire—he is God.

Elijah: Call on the name of your god, but do not light the fire.

Chorus 2: What you say is good. We have prepared the bull.

Ahab: Go on, prophets of Baal. Call on his name.

Chorus 2: O Baal, answer us!

Ahab: There is no answer. Shout louder.

Chorus 2: O Baal, answer us!

Ahab: There still is no answer. Shout louder and dance.

Chorus 2: O Baal, answer us!

Elijah: Shout louder! It's already noon, and you've been dancing and shouting for three hours. Surely he is a god who can hear you.

Chorus 2: O Baal, answer us!

Elijah: Maybe your god is busy. Maybe your god is too deep in thought. Maybe your god is asleep and needs to be awakened!

Chorus 2: O Baal, answer us!

Elijah: Maybe your god is traveling.

Chorus 2: O Baal, answer us!

Elijah: Yes, go on, you fools, slash yourselves with swords. Look at all that blood. Perhaps that will arouse the sympathy of your god.

Chorus 2: O Baal, answer us!

Elijah: Has no one answered you? Look, it's evening already. Come here to me, everyone.

Ahab: All right, Elijah. You've had your fun. Now, we'll have fun watching you pray like a fool to a god no one can touch or see or hear. It's your turn. Get your bull ready.

Elijah: My bull is ready; the altar is ready. Just to show you what kind of God I have, I'll make this even tougher. Pour four large jars of water on the altar.

Chorus 1: We have.

Elijah: Good. Pour more water.

Chorus 1: We have.

Elijah: Good. Pour more water.

Chorus 1: We have.

Elijah: See the water flow. Watch what my God can do. O Lord, God of Abraham, Isaac, and Israel. Let it be known today that you are God in Israel and that I am your servant. Answer me, O Lord, answer me, so these people will know that you, O Lord, are God and that you are turning their hearts back to you.

Ahab: Look at that fire fall from the sky! I can't believe it. The fire has burned up not only the bull but the wood, the stones, the soil, and the water! I fall on my knees.

Choruses 1 and 2: The Lord, he is God! The Lord—he is God!

Ahab: Your Lord, he is God.

Elijah: The Lord—he is my God!

Choruses 1 and 2: The Lord, he is my God!

Questions

- How do you think Elijah felt when he needed God's help for this big problem?
- Was this problem too big for God?
- How is this like the way you feel when you need God's help for a big problem?
- Is God big enough for your problem?

Story Extension Ideas

- Let kids make a big banner out of felt and shiny red, orange, and yellow fabric. Cut out letters that read, "The Lord—he is God!" You may glue or sew the letters on. Hang it on your class wall, or take your reading and your banner on the road to another class.
- Construct a fence out of several boards. Paint the fence, and write on it, "Get off the fence. If the Lord is God, follow him." (1 Kings 18:21) Call on the kids to check out the facts and, if they are ready, make a commitment. Today is the day of salvation.

Other Story Possibilities

- To tell a Crowd Out Loud tale, choose a biblical narrative with plenty of dialogue. Have the kids join you in writing the script. The song of Moses (Deuteronomy 32) is a brief but beautiful review of Israel's history. Intersperse Deuteronomy 32:3-4 between portions of it.
- The Last Supper could become a moving account told in this way. See Luke 22. Weave the verse, "This is my blood which is poured out for you" throughout the tale.

2-3

Unroll a Scroll

Children will make their own scrolls out of sticks, paper, and tape. They will act as scribes writing the story on their scrolls. The story is experienced when the kids find the scrolls hidden in church. They line up and read the complete story of a man of true character and conviction—Josiah—who did what was right in the eyes of the Lord.

The Story

Josiah's Book of the Law, 2 Kings 22–23:25

The Point

Follow God with all your heart.

The Materials

Sticks, tape, paper, scissors, pencils, a box to put the scrolls into, and photocopies of the handout titled "Josiah and the Holy Scrolls" (p. 67)

Preparation

If possible, let the children hunt outdoors for sticks to make their scrolls out of. They can cut paper to the width of the sticks and tape the papers together and then to the sticks to complete a scroll. Photocopy the story below, and divide and highlight the passages so that each child has a paragraph to attach to his or her scroll. There are thirteen paragraphs. Double up portions for a smaller class; divide the paragraphs for a larger class. Number the scrolls chronologically. If possible, find a wooden box or chest, and decorate it with jewels. Place some fake coins on top. Hide all the scrolls in the box. Hide the box in an empty sanctuary, if available, and let the children hunt for the box.

Directions

When the children find the box, have them each take a scroll and then line up according to the numbers on their scrolls. Read the introduction to them; then have them read the remainder of the story aloud from their own scrolls.

Introduction

When Josiah was born, his country, Judah, was a mess. The people had turned from God to idols. Idols are fake gods—statues that people worship. God had warned his people over and over to turn from idols and worship only him. Josiah had listened to stories about his neighboring country Israel. People in Israel had worshipped idols and had been dragged away by enemies. God takes idols very seriously. He knows that anything that comes between you and God needs to go. Josiah's father, King Amon, and his grandfather before him, King Manasseh, had been very evil kings. They worshipped fake idols. Manasseh made his own sons pass through fire to show how much he loved his idols. He even killed people who worshipped the true God. God was angry—very angry. And then Josiah became the king of Judah. What kind of king would he be? We'll find out.

Let's Begin

See the handout on page 67.

Questions

- How did Josiah feel when he discovered the scroll of God's Word?
- Why isn't it always easy to follow God?
- What are some ways you can follow and obey God?

Story Extension Ideas

- Make scrolls to unroll and eat! Let the kids take two pretzel sticks and a length of roll-up type fruit. Have them wrap the ends around the pretzels, roll, unroll, and enjoy the sweetness of God's Word.
- Josiah's total commitment challenges the most complacent of us today. Play a game called Right or Left (2 Kings 22:2). Have the kids cut out paper footprints and tape them to the floor in a long line. They can take turns walking straight on the path while other kids try to entice them to turn off the path with attractive offers. Also, show the kids with these footsteps that no matter how many steps they take away from God, it only takes one to get back to him!

Other Story Possibilities

- Other stories about God's Word can be printed out in portions, copied onto scrolls, and then shared aloud. The story of Jesus' proclamation in the synagogue that "Today this Scripture is fulfilled in your hearing" can be read and even acted out. See Luke 4:13-30.
- Another story about scrolls and total commitment is told in Acts 19:17-22. Have the children transcribe the story about Paul in Ephesus and the burning of the scrolls. "In this way, the Word of the Lord spread widely and grew in power."

JOSIAH AND THE HOLY SCROLLS

(1) Josiah became the king of Judah when he was only eight years old. He did what was right in the eyes of the Lord and walked in ways that pleased God. While he was still young, he began to truly follow God.

(2) King Josiah said, "I will fix God's church, the Temple." He collected money and paid men to repair the Temple. While one man was pouring the money out of a chest, he saw something inside. What could it be?

(3) He picked it up. It was a scroll. He unrolled it and gasped. He yelled, "I have found the Book of the Law in the Temple of the Lord!" He ran to the priest.

(4) "I found the Bible, the holy Scriptures from long ago!" The priest was so excited he began to shake. They ran to the king and read the scroll to King Josiah.

(5) Josiah listened to God's Word. It said, "Love the Lord your God. Do not follow other gods. If you worship other gods, the Lord will destroy you." (See Deuteronomy 6–7.)

(6) King Josiah knew they were in trouble. Many people in his land worshipped idols. Josiah turned white with terror.

(7) King Josiah was so upset, he ripped his fancy robe. He wept. He cried, "The Lord's anger burns against us. We have not obeyed him!"

(8) Wasting no time, King Josiah read the scroll of God's' Word to the priests and people. All the people decided to give their hearts to God. What a day!

(9) Josiah began to get rid of the idols in Judah. He tore down the places where they worshipped Baal, a fake god of rain and crops. King Josiah smashed their fancy idols.

(10) Josiah broke all the statues of their fake gods. He burned the bones of the men who were the idol teachers. He crushed their idols into powder.

(11) Josiah went wild for God. He cut to pieces all the places where the people burned spices to their fake gods. He went everywhere getting rid of these idols.

(12) Nothing could stop that man. He destroyed all the idols and the priests of the idols, too. He even held a huge Passover, a special holiday for God.

(13) There was never a king like King Josiah, not before or after him, who turned to the Lord as he did—with all his heart and with all his soul and with all his strength. Was Josiah a good king? You bet he was! The best!

2-3

Smarty Arty Party

All that your second- and third-graders need for this magical method of storytelling are paper, pencil, and some imagination. Don't worry if you lack some of that—the children will have plenty of creativity to lend you. Read this little-known story of King Nebuchadnezzar's exile into insanity. The kids will draw the crazy king while you describe him.

The Story

Nebuchadnezzar's Lunch, Daniel 4:1-37

The Point

God wants us to have a humble spirit.

The Materials

For each child: 11x14 paper, pencil, eraser, and markers or crayons

Preparation

Try to draw your own crazy king according to the tale below.

Directions

Define the word "humble" for the children. Fold each piece of paper in half and in half again so the paper has four areas for drawing. While you slowly describe each scene, the kids draw their version of the story. Allow plenty of time for the kids to draw between scenes. Complete the story, and let the children compare their funny drawings with one another.

Let's Begin

King Nebuchadnezzar of Babylon had everything. He had a mighty kingdom, riches, servants, power, everything, except...a humble spirit. This story tells how he received even that.

One day King Nebuchadnezzar was lying on his bed in his palace, fat and happy. He fell asleep and had a nightmare that struck terror in his heart. So the king called all the magicians, astrologers, and wise men in the kingdom to the palace. He begged them to tell him what his dream meant. But not one of them could figure it out.

Then Daniel came to the king. Daniel was a servant of the true God. King Nebuchadnezzar said, "Daniel, I know the spirit of the holy gods lives inside you. Please, tell me what my dream means. I dreamed about an enormous tree. The tree grew so large and strong that its top touched the sky. Its leaves were beautiful, and it had much delicious fruit hanging on it. Under the tree, animals found shelter, and the birds of the air lived in its branches. *(Pause here to let the children draw this scene in the first area of their papers.)*

"But then in my dream, an angel came down from heaven. He called in a loud voice, 'Cut down the tree and trim off its branches; strip off its leaves, and scatter its fruit. Let the animals and birds flee from the tree. *(Pause here to let the children draw this scene on the next area of their paper.)*

'Let him be covered with dew and let him live with the animals among the plants of the earth. Let his mind be changed from that of a man and let him be given the mind of an animal. Let him stay that way for seven years.'"

So Daniel told the king what the dream meant, for God told Daniel the meaning of the dream. Daniel said, "O King, if only this dream would become true about your enemies. You, O king, are that tree! You have become great and strong. Your kingdom stretches to the far parts of the earth. But you will be driven away from people and will live with the wild animals; you will eat grass like cattle and be drenched with dew. Seven years will pass before you can say that God is the true king and ruler. Then you will become the king again. So, please, O King, take my advice and repent. Stop your sins and start being kind."

Daniel had spoken the truth to the king, which was a risky thing. King Nebuchadnezzar could have chopped his head off for that. But he didn't harm Daniel. The king may even have been humbled—for a little while.

But time passed, a year to be exact, and the king slipped back into his selfish ways. One day King Nebuchadnezzar was walking on the roof of the royal palace. He looked out over his kingdom, to the thick and mighty fortresses. People busily scurried about doing his work. The fertile fields beyond were ripe. His world-famous gardens sent a whiff of jasmine into his nostrils. "Aahh," the king said. "Is not this the great Babylon I have built as the royal home by my mighty power and for the glory of my majesty?" *(Pause here to let the children add this scene to the next area of their papers.)*

Uh-oh. The words were still on his lips when a voice came from heaven, "King Nebuchadnezzar, your royal power has been taken from you. You will be driven away from people and live with the wild animals. You will eat grass like cattle. Seven years will pass before you admit that God is King of the world."

Immediately it happened. He was driven away.

Now, we're going to use our imaginations to draw King Nebuchadnezzar in his field. As I describe the king, you will draw him. If you'd like to share how you think he looked, we can add that to our drawing, too. The king became like a cow, crawling through the field on all fours. His hair grew like feathers of an eagle, all over his body. He couldn't shave, so his hair became thick and knotted, matted with dew. Thorns from the forest were entangled in his long, twisted, black beard. His wild, crazy eyes were constantly darting around. He had to beware of dangerous animals. His mouth was stuffed with grass. He had cuts on his face from fighting with a wild cat. His nails grew long, sharp, and curly, like the claws of a bird. Sometimes he hid behind bushes, trees, or rocks. He lived in a grassy field filled with tall weeds.

King Nebuchadnezzar lived like this for seven years. Finally, he raised his eyes toward heaven. He praised God. He told the Lord that God's kingdom lasts forever, that people of the earth, even himself, are nothing compared to God.

Just then, the king became normal! He was no longer insane. He was even allowed to be the king again and sit on the throne. His kingdom became even greater, but this time it was different. This time the king realized who the true King is. Nebuchadnezzar learned a tough lesson. He learned that, those who walk in pride, God is able to humble.

Questions

- In the beginning of the story, how did the king feel about the wealth and power God had given him?
- Why does God want us to be humble?
- When it is hard for you to be humble?
- How can you have Jesus help you with this area?

Story Extensions

- Make simple prayer journals with the children from folded paper and a construction paper cover. Let them draw a situation they would like God's help with and leave room to draw God's answer to the prayers.
- Turn Daniel 4:34-37 into a prayer. Insert God's name into the pronouns. Have children each acknowledge and thank God for positive attributes in their personality and lives.

Other Story Possibilities

- Let the children draw their rendition of the Temple as you read portions of 1 Kings 6–7. You may even want to add silver and gold pens for a special touch.
- There are beautiful images of heaven described in Revelation 4:2-6. In addition to drawing this, see if the children can find other descriptions of heaven in their Bibles.

K-1

Action Impaction

Take the pain out of listening, and put the wiggle back in! The children look at simple pictures on cue cards for actions to perform while you tell the story. Throughout the story, you'll hold up different cards and have the children act them out. A group of any size will have a roarin' good time learning about Daniel and the lions.

The Story

Daniel in the Lions' Den, Daniel 6

The Point

Stand up for your faith.

The Materials

Three pieces of poster board and a marker

Preparation

Draw a crown on one piece of poster board, praying hands on another, and a lion's open jaws and jagged teeth on a third. You needn't be an artist. Children have big imaginations.

Directions

When you see the word "**king**" in bold, hold up the crown picture. Tell the children that when they see the crown, they have to bow. Any time you see the word "**pray**" in bold, hold up the picture of the hands. The kids have to kneel down in a prayer position momentarily. When you see the word "**lion**" in bold, hold up the lion picture, and have the kids growl and show their teeth.

Let's Begin

Have you ever been hungry? really hungry? mouth-watering, stomach-growling, teeth-grinding hungry? Some lions were that hungry. And they were served an old man for dinner! This is a story about the pride of a king and a pride of lions. You are going to help me tell the story.

(Explain the cards. Tell the kids they can say each word with you.)

King Darius was like a **lion**. His army had taken over the city of Babylon, and now he needed rulers. So the **king** looked for three smart men. One of them was named Daniel.

Daniel was a good, honest hard worker, so the **king** thought, "I'll put Daniel in charge of my whole kingdom."

Well, when the other princes and rulers heard about the plan, they were mad. So these men tried to catch Daniel doing something wrong. They tried to catch Daniel in a lie, but he never lied. They tried to catch Daniel stealing, but Daniel didn't steal. They even tried to catch Daniel being lazy, but Daniel worked hard.

Those mad princes got madder. "Rrrats," screamed one of them. "The only way we'll ever get rid of Daniel is if it has something to do with his God."

"Good idea. Daniel **prays**!" a prince said, stroking his beard. The men whispered and planned and plotted and laughed. Then they went to the **king** with their idea.

"O, **King** Darius, live forever! You are so wise and great and wonderful that we think there should be a new law. The new law will say that if anyone **prays** to any god or man, except to YOU, for the next thirty days, he will be thrown into the **lions**' den!"

Darius thought about it. Hhhhmmm. It sounded pretty good to him. His big fat pride got bigger and fatter. "Okay," he said and signed the law.

Now when Daniel learned about the new law, he went home to **pray**. In the morning, at noon, and at night, three times a day, every day, Daniel knelt down, and **prayed** out loud to his God.

Would he today? Would Daniel disobey the **king**? Would he **pray** to this strange God of his, the people wondered. Why would he risk his life for this God of the air—a God you couldn't see or touch? If he did pray to this invisible God, could this God answer? Surely this God wasn't stronger than the powerful jaws of a **lion**. Or was he?

It was almost noon. Tick, tick, dong. Sure enough, Daniel sat near his window to **pray.** He got down on his knees and **prayed**, giving thanks to his God, just as he had done before. Who do you think was there, listening as Daniel begged God for help? Yes, the jealous rulers.

They ran to the **king** and said, "We found someone who broke your law!"

The **king** jumped to his feet, furious. "Who is it? I'll throw him to the **lions**!"

"We thought you'd never ask," the princes smiled, "It's Daniel."

Darius went white. He fell back into his throne. "Daniel?" he said in a weak voice, "Not Daniel. Why, it just can't be. Whose stupid law was this anyway? You tricked me! I'm the **king.** I'll just change the law, that's all." Darius tried until sundown to find a way to save Daniel, but he couldn't.

"Remember, this law can't be changed," the princes said wagging their fingers.

So the **king** gave the order to throw Daniel into the **lions'** den. Those **lions** were hungry. They hadn't been fed for days. You could see their ribs sticking to their skin. They licked their chops, drooling for meat. As Daniel was thrown down into the deep pit, you could hear the **lions** growling.

A stone was placed over the mouth of the den. Darius shouted, "Daniel, may your God, whom you serve continually, rescue you." And the **king** returned to his palace. Poor **King** Darius. He didn't eat anything for dinner that night. He didn't even want singers to sing or jugglers to juggle or dancers to dance for him. Poor **King** Darius. He couldn't sleep all night long.

Meanwhile in the dark, black pit, Daniel heard the **lions** pace back and forth, their tails swishing, their teeth grinding. He could smell them; they could smell him. They got closer. Did he try to kick the **lions** or find a rock to defend himself? Not Daniel. He **prayed**. And he **prayed**. GGRrrrr, Ggggrrr, ggrrr. Purr. Meow.

At the first morning light, the **king** ran to the den. As he peered down into the darkness, did he see Daniel's ripped clothes? Did he see the morning light shining on Daniel's bones? No. He called to Daniel in a worried voice, "Daniel, servant of the living God, has your God, whom you serve continually, been able to rescue you from the **lions**?"

For a moment, there was only silence. And then the **king** heard the most wonderful sound his ears could hear. It was Daniel's strong, clear voice saying, "O **King**, live forever! My God sent his angel, and he shut the mouths of the **lions**!"

The **king** was overjoyed. When Daniel was lifted out of the den, not one scratch was found on him because he had trusted in his God. Those tricky rulers were thrown into the den. The **lions** tore them to pieces before they even touched the ground, crushing all their bones.

Darius wrote letters to people in every land telling them to praise God, Daniel's God, because he is the real **King** who lives forever. He can do miracles, even rescue Daniel from the jaws of hungry **lions**.

Questions

- How do you think Daniel felt in the lion's den?
- Why did Daniel trust God?
- If Daniel could trust God while hungry lions prowled around him, what can you trust God for?

Story Extensions

- Encourage the children to choose a prayer window in their home. They can make a window out of construction paper that opens to the verse, "Three times a day he got down on his knees and prayed, giving thanks to his God, just as he had done before." Daniel 6:10b. Or they can trace their hands inside the window and write the verse on the shutters.
- Play the Lion Tame Game. Form a lion's pit on a large area, either grassy or carpeted. Choose one Daniel, and let the other kids be lions. Have lions be close to the pit. The lions must prowl back and forth along the edge of the pit while Daniel tries to escape from them. If a lion brushes up against Daniel, he becomes the next Daniel.

Other Story Possibilities

Choose simple stories with few elements or characters.

- Samuel's Summons. Draw a picture of a boy asleep, Samuel's name, and a boy awake to actively tell this tale. Be sure to let the children act it out afterwards. See 1 Samuel 3.
- Peter escapes from prison in Acts 12:1-19. Use the prayer hands, and draw a chain and an angel for the picture clue cards. The action for chains can be two fists crossed at the chest, and the angel can be symbolized with hands over the head forming a halo.

K-3

Motion Commotion

Mastering this teaching technique will have a lasting impact on your ministry. Teaching with movement sparks a positive learning cycle when you see the children respond enthusiastically. Teaching with echoes and motions is perfect for a large group, "a vast army."

The Story

Valley of Bones, Ezekiel 37:1-14

The Point

God can do anything!

The Materials

A Bible, a bone, (real or cut from paper), a chain or keys to rattle, and poster board

Preparation

Read the script over once.

Directions

The boldfaced words are what the children are to echo. After reading the boldfaced phrase, point to the children.

Let's Begin

Do you like scary stories? Did you know that the most exciting and even the most frightening and dreadful stories in the world are told right here? *(Hold up your Bible.)* In your Bible. This story is about skeletons, graves, and a nightmare that a man named Ezekiel had. Listen to this bone-chilling, future-filling, hope-thrilling story. You can help me tell it by just doing what I say. When I point to you, you echo what I just said.

Ezekiel was a prophet. A prophet is a person who speaks God's words. What is a prophet? A prophet is **a person who speaks God's words**. What is a prophet? **A prophet is a person who speaks God's words.** Ezekiel was a **prophet**. Ezekiel was a prophet in Babylon. God's people, the Jews, had not obeyed God. So God took all the Jewish people out of their homeland of Judah and brought them into a strange new country. This made the Jewish people very *(Make a sad face.)* **sad.** They loved Jerusalem and wanted to go home, but they had to finish their time out in this foreign country that didn't believe in or worship the true God.

But God gave the prophet Ezekiel a wild dream. God gave him a nightmare in the middle of the day to show God's people that **God can do anything,** even take them home. You can pretend to be Ezekiel. Close your eyes and lie down. *(Turn out the lights and whisper.)* While Ezekiel was sleeping, God picked him up and carried him over the city walls, past the hanging gardens and through the desert. He plopped Ezekiel down in a valley, surrounded by mountains. *(Turn on the lights.)* Wake up and stand up.

Ezekiel looked out into the valley. He saw all these white things lying around out in the field. *(Shade your eyes and let the kids copy you.)* What were they? Ezekiel stepped closer. Come on; step closer. He reached down and picked one up. Could it be…? *(Reach down and pick up a bone. Look at it. Drop it.)* Hah, a bone! Not just one bone, **thousands of bones**! **Dry, white, human bones,** scattered everywhere as though there had been a terrible war years ago. All of the skin and muscles were gone!. A thighbone was lying next to a skull, a rib cage next to some arm bones. Ezekiel walked back and forth among the bones. Then he heard the voice of God ask him, "Son of man, can these bones live?"

What do you kids think? Can dead, dry bones live? *(Let children answer.)* No. No. No!

Ezekiel answered, "**O mighty Lord,** you alone know that."

God said to Ezekiel, "Tell the bones, '**Dry bones, hear the word of the Lord!** I will make you come to life Then you will know that I am the Lord.'"

So Ezekiel said to the bones, **"Dry bones, hear the word of the Lord**, **I will make you come to life**. **Then you will know that I am the Lord."**

Now, you are each going to pretend to be pieces of bones. Lie down without touching each other. You can be a foot bone. You can be a finger bone. You can be a skull. *(Point to different children.)* While I rattle a chain [or keys], you slowly shake your decayed bones. Stand up. Then hold someone's hand as though the bones are coming together, piece by piece, so that everyone is joined together.

So Ezekiel said, *(Start rattling chain.)* **"Dry bones, come together, bone to bone."** He heard a sound. The bones were rattling in the wind, finding each other and turning themselves into complete human skeletons. *(Stop rattling chain.)* Keep your head down. You are still a lifeless skeleton.

Then an amazing thing happened. Muscles started to wrap around the bones. Still hearts, empty stomachs, and hollow lungs began to appear on the flesh. Then the muscles suddenly were dressed in skin! Still the bodies didn't move. *(Whisper.)* They were perfectly still and perfectly quiet, like lifeless toy soldiers.

Then God said to Ezekiel, **"Talk to the wind.** Tell the wind, 'Come, four winds, and breathe breath into these dead bodies that they may live. Then you will know that I am the Lord.'" And that is what Ezekiel did.

He said, **"Come, four winds,** and **breathe breath into these dead bodies** that they may live. **Then you will know that I am the**

Lord." *(Wave a poster board back and forth.)* Swallow your wind, bodies. And breath entered the bodies. They came to life and stood up on their feet. The dead valley was now filled with **a vast, living army.** *(Have the children lift up their heads and salute.)*

God told Ezekiel, "See what I can do? I can bring pieces of a skeleton together and turn them into a living, breathing human being. **I will bring you home.** Now you will know that I, **the Lord, can do anything!**"

That is what happened. Ezekiel woke up. The Jewish people eventually came home. They realized that **God can do anything**.

Questions

- How do you think Ezekiel felt when the bones were made into a vast army?
- Tell about something fantastic God has done in your life or for someone you know.
- Is there something in your life that seems too hard for you? How can you give it to God to handle?

Story Extension Ideas

- Read Ezekiel 37:12-14. Now read Matthew 27:50-54. Why did God bring the dead to life? Make a skeleton out of white paper, and attach each bone with a brass fastener. Have the children put Ezekiel 37:4-6 in their own words on the skeleton.
- Make a new-life cake. Bury a plastic butterfly in cake batter and bake. Decorate with white frosting tinted green and green sprinkles. Also add small flower decorations, and add a large butterfly cut from a plastic foam plate with "Jesus gives new life" written on it.

Other Story Possibilities

To use repetition and motion, first look for active verbs that can be translated into simple motions. Then look for phrases for them to echo. Intersperse echoes and motion.

- The story of the golden calf, found in Exodus 32, is full of kinetic verbs. Have the kids look up the mountain for Moses, shrug their shoulders wondering where he is, and cast their pretend jewelry into the fire.
- Elijah fed by the ravens (1 Kings 17) will entice the kids to echo the Lord's edict, imitate ravens, and hide from the ill-tempered Ahab.

K-5

Crazy Clothesline Characters

This may be the wildest of all the wonderful ways to tell a story. Stretch a clothesline across the room, and hang outfits on it for the different characters from the book of Esther. You will jump from behind one outfit to the next for speedy clothing changes while presenting the story according to the script. This may not be a method for a shy teacher, but it will entertain and educate audiences of all sizes and ages.

The Story

Esther

The Point

God's purposes will prevail.

The Materials

Photocopies of the handout titled "Queen Esther" (pp. 79-80); outfits for a king, a queen, Esther, Haman, and Mordecai (you can include a white beard made of synthetic fiber); clothesline and clothespins, and jewels. (Persian royalty used a lot of jewelry, even the men.) Optional props: goblet spray-painted gold, scroll made of paper and two sticks, black material

Preparation

You will need two adults, one for the narrator and the other to play all the other parts, preferably someone who will ham it up. Photocopy the handouts for the storyteller and the narrator. Prepare the outfits. These can be real dresses, robes, and so on, or they can be made of poster board. If you make the outfits out of poster board, decorate them with imitation jewelry. Hang the outfits at the proper height for the actor's head to appear when he or she stands behind them. Practice at least once. If you are using adult clothing, the clothesline can get heavy, so get two strong adult helpers to hold either end of the clothesline during the story.

Directions

The actor will move from costume to costume for each different character. Esther can use Queen Vashti's outfit when Esther becomes the queen. After the clothes are ready, bring in the audience to see this fast-paced, funny tale. Use appropriate voice changes to add reality and humor. The king is rather obnoxious, Esther is gracious, Haman is sly and snarling, and Mordecai is old and wise. The narrator can hand the props to the actor.

Let's Begin

See the handout on pages 79-80.

Questions

- How do you think Esther felt knowing that God had used her to save the Jews?
- Can you share about a time when you saw God's plans working in your life?
- What plans do you think God has for your life?

Story Extension Ideas

- Study Esther 4:14b: "And who knows but that you have come to royal position for such a time as this?" Have the students each draw a map, placing their name (or their photo) in the center. They can draw a school and put the names of friends inside, homes of neighbors, or places they visit. Have the kids think of the people in their lives and for what special purposes they could be there.
- Talk about God's perfect timing in this story. Have older kids look up the following stories: The Pharaoh's daughter **happened** to bath in the Nile when baby Moses went floating by (Exodus 2:5). Jesus **happened** to glance up to see Peter when the rooster crowed (Luke 22:61). Isaac's servant **happened** to find Rebekah at the well (Genesis 24). Have the kids think of more Bible stories to illustrate this concept, such as Jonah, King Saul in the cave, and so on. Watch the clock, and have one child stand up and share one story every minute. This will imprint God's omnipotence in their minds.

Other Story Possibilities

- You can use these clothes and some variations to tell many Bible stories. King Agrippa and Queen Bernice were the recipients of a beautiful testimony Paul gave. You would need to make some chains for Paul (Acts 25–26).
- The story of the queen of Sheba and King Solomon, told in 1 Kings 10 and 2 Chronicles 9, is simple and straightforward. Have the children come up with questions from the queen of Sheba and use Solomon's answers from the book of Proverbs.

QUEEN ESTHER

Narrator: The book of Esther tells a fascinating story about a selfish king drunk with power, a beautiful queen hiding a secret, and a jealous prime minister bent on murder. It takes place in the kingdom of Persia about five hundred years before Christ. This is the story of how God's plans won and the Jewish people were saved.

King Xerxes: (*Holding up a golden goblet*) Come one; come all! Everyone in my royal palace, come join my grand celebration. Feast your stomachs on my tasty food. Feast your eyes upon my lovely gardens. Drool over my riches. Let yourself be dazzled with my wealth. Look, even my couches are made of silver, gold, pearls, and jewels. Come drink with me. Even my goblets for drinking are made of pure gold. And you should see my wife. Queen Vashti is, of course, the most lovely creature in the kingdom. Hey, somebody bring me my queen. I want to show her off.

Haman: Queen Vashti, your husband, King Xerxes, requests your presence at his celebration.

Queen Vashti: No. No way.

Haman: (*Clears throat.*) Pardon me, Your Majesty. Perhaps you did not understand me. Your husband, the KING, is telling you to come to his party!

Queen Vashti: Read my lips: No! I refuse to prance around in front of that group of drunken fools.

Haman: (*Whistling*) Okaaay. *(To the king)* I am sorry, Your Most Excellent Excellency. The queen said no.

King Xerxes: What? She said NO? No one says NO to me! I'm the king! (*Yelling*) What am I supposed to do now?

Haman: Sir, if you want my advice, get rid of her, and find a more worthy queen.

King Xerxes: Hmmm, good idea. Find me the most gorgeous woman in the entire kingdom. Better yet, find me every beautiful woman in the kingdom, and I'll pick my favorite! Ha, ha! Maybe this won't be so bad after all!

Narrator: And so it was. Every beautiful young woman was brought into the king's palace. Now the king had a guard who sat at his gate named Mordecai. Mordecai was a Jew. He worshipped the true God. He had a cousin named Esther. When Mordecai heard about the king's search for a new queen, he rushed home.

Mordecai: Esther, the king is searching for a new queen. He wants to see all the beautiful girls in the kingdom, so of course, I thought of you.

Esther: The king would never want me. I'm a Jew.

Mordecai: You wouldn't have to tell him. Just think. You have a chance to be queen of the entire empire!

Esther: Well, if this could possibly be God's plan for my life, I'll try it.

Narrator: And so Esther was brought to the king's palace. It was swarming with gorgeous women from all over the kingdom. They stared at each other, thinking, "Is she prettier than I?" Oh, you could smell perfume drifting out the windows. The women were treated to special baths, food, makeup, jewelry, and fancy dresses. Finally, it was Esther's turn to see the king. When Esther walked through the palace, all heads turned and people gasped. She seemed to glow with dignity, beauty, and charm. She held her head high and hid her secret in her heart. A Jew become the queen?

Haman: Your Excellency, we now present Esther from the province of Susa.

King Xerxes: (*Jaw drops, big gulp.*) Where have you been hiding her? She is without a doubt the finest woman in the kingdom. Let's have a celebration. I've found my new queen!

Esther: I am honored, Your Majesty.

Narrator: So a little Jewish girl who was raised without a father or mother became queen of the most powerful empire on earth. Now, the king decided to honor Haman. At the king's command, all the people and even the royal workers were to kneel down to pay honor to Haman.

Haman: What's your problem, Mordecai, you Jew.

Can't you see everyone bowing down to me? Get down on your knees!

Modecai: Never. I bow only before the Lord God Almighty.

Haman: Oohh, you slime. You'll pay for that! King Xerxes, there are some scum in your kingdom—the Jews. They're real troublemakers. They think they are better than we are, and they won't obey you, Your Royal Majesty. If it pleases you, make a law to destroy these Jewish rebels.

King Xerxes: Very well.

Haman: Now, just sign here. (*Unroll the scroll.*) It says...bbbzzz we will kill, destroy, annihilate all the Jews—young and old, men, women, and little children—on the thirteenth day of the twelfth month. And of course, we get all their stuff, ha, ha, ha...

King Xerxes: Oh, Haman, you are a wonder. Let's have a drink.

Haman: (*Rubbing hands*) Oh, yes, sire. Let's drink...to increasing your kingdom by decreasing the Jews. Ha, ha, ha, ha!

Esther: What! All the Jews are to be killed? It can't be! What can I do? I'm not allowed to talk to the king unless he invites me. If I do, he will put me to death.

Mordecai: If you remain silent, God will help us somehow. But think about it, Esther. Perhaps God made you the queen for this very purpose, to save your people.

Esther: Very well. Tell all God's people to pray for me. For three days, have them eat and drink nothing. I will do the same. I will go before the king and beg him to save the Jews. If I die, I die.

Narrator: After three days of fasting and prayer, Queen Esther was ready. She put on her royal robes and sat near the king's throne, hoping he would notice her. He did. She invited him to come to a banquet along with Haman. Haman went home bragging...

Haman: I get to eat with the king AND queen tomorrow. Man, am I it or what? The only thing that gets to me is that stupid Mordecai. He won't bow down to me, and it drives me crazy! What? Great idea, my wife. I'll build a tall tower to hang Mordecai! Then everyone in the kingdom will see! Ha, ha, ha...I'll have it built today.

Narrator: Haman had the tall tower built. The next day Queen Esther invited the king and Haman to a royal banquet. After a delicious dinner, the king said...

King Xerxes: What is it you would like, my beautiful queen? I will give you anything, even up to half my kingdom.

Esther: Please, O King, spare my life and the life of my people. All of the Jews are supposed to be killed on the thirteenth day! Please change the law.

King Xerxes: What? Who dared think of such a horrid law?

Esther: That man, the wicked Haman.

King Xerxes: Haman! You tricked me. I'm walking out of this room before I kill you with my own two hands.

Haman: Queen Esther, I beg, you spare my life. The king will kill me. Waaahhh.

Narrator: It was no use. Some royal officials covered Haman's face with a black veil. The king looked out the window and saw the tower that Haman had built to hang Mordecai on.

King Xerxes: Hang Haman on his own tower!

Narrator: And so the evil Haman was hanged on his own tower, and the Jews were saved. With joy, they had a great feast. And when the other people in the kingdom saw God's mighty power at work for the Jews, many of them became Jews. It became a holiday, and the Jews still celebrate a God whose plans prevail.

K-1

Big Figures

This technique allows all the children to be involved with little practice. The children make big figures out of poster board and hold them up while you recite a whimsical, fast-paced poem. Even shy kids don't mind performing because they can "hide" behind the figures.

The Story

Jonah and the Fish, Jonah 1–4

The Point

God wants us to obey.

Materials

Blue, tan, white, and brown poster board; markers or paint; a paint stir stick; a stapler, duct tape, and a piece of material for Jonah's tunic. Optional: large rolling craft eyes for Jonah and the whale

Preparation

Cut out large shapes of Jonah, a large fish, a boat, a sail, and waves from the appropriate colors of poster board. If you want to add additional pieces for other children, you can cut out small fishes, the city of Ninevah, signs for Ninevah and Tarshish, or the people of Ninevah.

Directions

Let the children color or paint the poster pieces. Add the cloth to Jonah with a stapler. Use duct tape to attach the paint stir stick to the sail, and then tape the sail to the boat. Explain the words "content" and "repent" to the children. Have the children each practice holding their figure and stepping forward when their character is mentioned. They then step back and lower the figure. You may have to point to them as well. Make sure they add motion when needed, such as Jonah running, waves rolling, and the boat rocking.

Let's Begin

God said, "Go, **Jonah**, go to the people by the sea."
Jonah said, "No, Lord, no! You can't mean me!"
"It's you I want to go, go, GO."

Jonah said, "I will not go, Lord, no, no, NO."
So he ran away, and he jumped on a **boat**.
But God wouldn't let that big **boat** float.

The men on the boat were afraid of the motion.
So they picked **Jonah** up and threw him in the ocean.
Down through the water did Jonah fall,
And then he said, "I know who I'll call.
"Help me, Lord. This is my wish!"
So God sent Jonah into a great big **fish**.
It was dark in the **fish**, but Jonah saw the light.
With his God he could not fight.
"Yes, Lord, yes, I will go
to tell the people who do not know
how big and wide and deep and tall
is God's love for us all."
So that great big fish spit **Jonah** out.
He ran to the **people** and began to shout,
"Turn to God and repent, repent!"
The **people** did. So was God content?
Yes, he was. Was Jonah glad?
No. In fact he was a little bit mad.
Jonah, Jonah, do you still not see?
(All)
That God loves everyone,
Including me.

Questions

- How did Jonah feel about obeying God?
- Can you share a time when you had to do something you didn't want to do?
- How will you act the next time you are asked to do a job that you don't feel like doing?

Story Extension Ideas

- Parents will love to watch their youngsters perform this fishy tale. The audience participates with rhythmic clapping.
- Make boats out of bagels. For a sail, tape a triangular-shaped piece of paper to a toothpick. Let a teddy bear cookie serve as Jonah. The children will eat up the story!

Other Story Possibilities

You can tell almost any Bible story with big, simple figures. Don't worry if you aren't an artist, the kids will fill in the missing details with their imaginations. For story text, simply tell the Bible story in your words. Or the children could help you put the story into their own words. There are many songs, poems, and picture books that tell Bible tales, so keep your eyes and ears peeled for possibilities.

- From Daniel 3, Shadrach, Meshach, Abednego, a statue, and flames would tell the tale, with the figures refusing to bow. Don't forget to make the fourth figure hiding amid the flames—the Son of God.
- Jesus raising a widow's son from Luke 7:11-16 has wonderful possibilities.

New
Testament
Stories

K-1

Glad-to-Add Story

What to do with all those beautiful Christmas cards you accumulate each year? Use them to tell the story of Christ's birth. As the nativity story is told, the children can decide which card best illustrates that portion of the narrative. They take turns hanging the cards on a clothesline.

The Story

Jesus' Birth, Matthew 2:1-12 and Luke 2:1-20

The Point

Jesus is a special gift.

The Materials

A collection of used Christmas cards, (the more the merrier), a clothesline, clothespins, and a star for the top. Optional for ambiance: Christmas lights

Preparation

One week in advance, send a letter home with the children asking for old Christmas cards. Ask the parents to cut off the inside part of the card so that all you have is the picture. Before the class meets, hang a clothesline across one wall at a height that the children can easily reach. You may add a line of Christmas lights above this.

Directions

Let the children sort through the cards, separating the secular ones from the ones that tell the story of Jesus' birth. Set aside the secular cards. Let each child choose several cards to hold. While you tell the story, they each will decide if their cards show what you are describing. If one of their cards does, they quietly walk up to the line and use a clothespin to hang it up as the story progresses. Plug in the lights on the night Jesus is born.

Let's Begin

A King was coming! How busy the angels were those days making everything just right. The world didn't know it, but they were about to receive the best gift God could give—his Son. Did God send his own precious Son to be born to a rich queen? No. Did God send his Son to live in the fanciest, most lavish palace on earth? No.

God picked a young lady named Mary. Mary

loved God. One day the angel Gabriel appeared to Mary and said, "Greetings, the Lord is with you." Mary was greatly troubled. But the angel said, "Do not be afraid, Mary. God is pleased with you. You have been chosen to carry God's Son as your own. You will give birth to him and call him Jesus. He will be the King forever and save his people from their sins. Nothing is impossible with God."

Mary said, "I am the Lord's servant. May it be to me as you have said."

Mary promised to marry Joseph, a good man in Nazareth. One day Joseph came to her and said, "Mary, we have to take a trip to Bethlehem. The Emperor made a law that says we have to all be counted." And so Mary and Joseph made the long trip to Bethlehem. It wasn't easy because Mary had to ride on the back of a donkey and she was very pregnant. Up and down, side to side, back and forth. Oh, won't it feel good to get a nice room at the inn and stretch out, thought Mary.

Finally, they arrived in Bethlehem, tired, sore, and hungry. Joseph and Mary knocked on the door of the inn. But they were told to go away because the inn was already full. And so Mary and Joseph settled into a stable, where animals live. Imagine the King of the world being born in a dark and smelly stable. It may even have been like a cave. That night Jesus was born to our world. It was the very first Christmas. Waaahhh! His cry was music in a lonely, forgotten corner of the world. It was the happiest day of Mary and Joseph's life. The donkey heeed and hawed. A soft, woolly lamb cuddled next to the little Jesus. The cow's big brown eyes blinked as she looked at the little Lord. Mary wrapped her baby as cozy as she could with some strips of cloth. Joseph smiled and kissed Jesus.

Heaven burst with joy! Angel after angel after angel swooped down from their home in glory to tell the story. Their dazzling light filled the skies. And to whom did they race so they could share this good news? First, an angel appeared to some shepherds who were out watching their sheep. The shepherds were terrified when they saw the brilliant angel hovering in the sky above them. But the angel said, "Do not be afraid. I bring you good news of great joy that will be for all the people. Today a Savior has been born to you; he is Christ the Lord!"

Before the shepherds could believe their eyes or ears, the whole sky was shining with singing, shouting, glowing angels! They praised God with the first Christmas carol, "Glory to God in the highest!" And then, just like that, they disappeared into the night.

The shepherds must have looked at each other and said, "Were we dreaming?" But they ran into town to find this baby King. When the shepherds found him, they shared with everyone the amazing thing that happened to them.

(Turn the room lights low, and turn the Christmas lights on.) When you were born, your parents may have sent a special card to everyone they knew, telling them the good news of your birth. God sent something special for his Son, too. God sent a message for the whole world to see—a brilliant, dazzling star, shining down on the place where the baby Jesus stayed. The star beamed and danced in the sky as if silently shouting, "Come and see, come and see God wrapped up as a baby!" Three wise men followed the star from many miles on camel to see Jesus. Three wise men bowed down before a young King, God's Son, Jesus.

Questions

- How do you feel at Christmas when you open your gifts?
- How is this like the way the shepherds and the wise men felt about baby Jesus?
- How can you show how much you like the wonderful gift of Jesus?

Story Extension Ideas

- Fill lunch sacks with special Christmas cookies. Punch holes in the top of each bag, and attach a Christmas card as a tag. Go Christmas caroling to other classes or to a nursing home, and leave a bag as a Christmas gift.
- Play a game called Find Jesus with a flashlight and a baby doll. You can be the first one to hide the baby Jesus doll. The rest of the class can be the shepherds or wise men looking for baby Jesus. When baby Jesus is found, they can shine the light down on him.

Other Story Possibilities

The possibilities of ways to add on to a story are as endless as your imagination.

- Use pictures from nature magazines or old calendars to tell the story of Creation in Genesis 1.
- Hang small stuffed animals from the clothesline to help the children explore the story of Noah and the ark in Genesis 6–8.

K-3

Cue Cards

The children will respond in unison to cue cards, held up as the story unfolds. Audiences of all sizes will enjoy participating in this story of Jesus' temptation in the desert. It is presented as a boxing match in the ultimate battle of good versus evil.

The Story

Temptation of Jesus, Matthew 4:1-11 and Luke 4:1-13

The Point

Fight temptation with God's Word.

The Materials

A helper, poster board, and markers. Optional: bell or timer to ring, and a fake microphone

Preparation

Use markers to make the following cue cards on poster board: a drum, two hands clapping, a snake (hiss), a thumb pointing down (boo), and the word "No!" Get into the spirit of a sportscaster (How's your Howard Cosell voice?) as the battle heats up. Make a creepy voice for the devil.

Directions

Read the story aloud. Have a helper hold up the appropriate cue card as you read the story. Give the kids a chance to respond to the cue cards in the following way: When you hold up the snake card, they are to make a hissing sound. When you hold up the clapping hand card, they clap their hands. When you hold up the drum card, they'll drum on their knees. They can say "boo" for the thumb-down card and say the word "no" for the "No!" card. Practice once with the kids before the story, holding up the cards and turning them down as a signal to stop.

Let's Begin

Ladies and gentlemen, thank you for joining us in the desert wilderness of Judea. In this corner we have straight from the glories of heaven, **(drum)**, the Son of God, the Messiah, the only being that is fully God and fully human…the Lord Jesus Christ! **(hands)**

In this corner we have straight from the pit of hell **(drum)**, the archenemy of God, that great dragon, that ancient serpent, the father of all lies…the devil! **(thumb)**

Ladies and gentlemen, you are in for the fight of the century. We have the ultimate forces of good pitted against the ultimate forces of evil. Hold on to your chair as we begin. **(Ring a bell.)** Our story begins after the Lord Jesus Christ was baptized. Jesus was about to begin his mission. He was out to tell everyone about God's love, and the devil **(thumb)** was out to stop him dead in his tracks! The Holy Spirit of God led Jesus out into the desert to be tempted by the devil. Who will win this battle of the ages? Do any of us realize what is at stake? **(No!)**

(Ring a bell.) Let Round 1 begin. In this corner, we have the Son of God. Do you see huge, rippling muscles? **(No!)** You see his rib cage sticking to his skin. Jesus has gone without food for forty—count 'em—forty days. And he is hungry. Even the snakes and lizards slithering around him are starting to look delicious. The thorny scrubs offer little shade. He is tired, thirsty, lonely, and hungry. Do we have what looks like a winner here? **(No!)** We'll find out.

In this corner, we have Satan **(thumb)**, the devil himself. Does he come to tempt Jesus while he's strong and surrounded by his friends? **(No!)** He comes to tempt Jesus after he's gone forty days without food or friends. That slime will stop at nothing. Here comes the first hit. The devil is saying **(snake)**, "If you are the Son of God, tell these stones to become bread."

Ooh, that punch was definitely below the belt. **(thumb)** Satan hit Jesus where he hurt the most. Will the Son of God survive this perilous punch? **(drum)** He could easily make the stones become bread. Will Jesus topple to the devil's trick? Will he turn one stone into bread? Will Jesus use his power for himself? Will he eat before God tells him to? He's staggered back under the blow, but he's getting up. Shh, I can hardly hear him. **(drum)** Here comes the return punch. Jesus is actually hitting back with a Bible verse. He is saying, "It is written in the Bible: 'Man does not live on bread alone, but on every word that comes from the mouth of God.'"

Yes! **(clap)** Woo-hoo! Jesus returns an equally deadly blow using the force of the Word of God! Round 1 goes to Jesus Christ, the Son of God. **(hands)**

(Ring a bell.) Round 2. Satan **(thumb)** is taking Jesus to the holy city of Jerusalem. Now they are standing on the highest point of the Temple. What is that deadly deceiver up to now? Ladies and gentlemen, I've never seen a fight like this before—they are going at it outside the ring of the desert. The devil is hissing **(snake)**: "If you are the Son of God, throw yourself down. For the Bible says, 'He will command his angels and they will lift you up in their hands, so that you will not strike your foot against a stone.'"

Ooh, that dirty devil delivered a deadly blow, tempting him to jump from the top of the Temple **(thumb)**, using the Word of God to confuse the Savior. **(thumb)** Will the Son of God jump? Will God protect him? Will he amaze the crowds with this cheap magic trick?

Jesus looks over the top of the temple. **(drum)** There is a crowd of people below. He speaks: "It is also written in the Bible: 'Do not put the Lord your God to the test.'"

Yes! Brilliant! **(hands)** Jesus Christ fights Scripture with Scripture! He wins Round 2. Satan will stop at nothing, even twisting Scripture to destroy the Son of God. He was defeated at his own game. **(hands)** Does the devil give up? **(No!)** This battle between the Prince of Darkness and the Prince of Light continues.

(Ring a bell.) Round 3. What dirty deed is the devil up to now? **(thumb)** He is taking Jesus up to a very high mountain and showing him all the kingdoms of the world. **(drum)** Listen. He is saying **(snake)**, "All this I will give you if…**(drum)**…you will bow down and worship me."

Now that was low! That strike could be the deadly blow. Isn't that what Jesus came for, to be the King of the world? Satan is offering his control of the entire splendid universe for one moment of victory? Will the Son of God fall for this temptation? **(No!)** He has staggered back. **(drum)** Will Jesus bow to Satan? Will Jesus really turn his back on the mission his father has sent him on? Will Jesus worship Satan and scorn the cross to gain the world?

Quiet, ladies and gentlemen, Jesus is speaking. He's saying **(drum)**, "Away from me, Satan! For it is written in the Bible: 'Worship the Lord your God and serve him only.'"

Victory!! **(hands)** YES! Jesus Christ, the Holy Son of God, God in the flesh, and the Light of the World has won! Look at Satan slink away. He's defeated! **(hands)** Give the crown to Jesus. He has battled Satan at his weakest moments and won! He was tempted and won every round with a blow from Scripture. **(hands)** Ladies and gentlemen, I have never seen a fight like this before. Look at all the angels. There must be thousands of them coming to take care of Jesus. They've been holding their breath and rooting for Jesus, too. Stay tuned, boys and girls. The devil **(thumb)** will be back for another battle, and the next fighter will be…**(drum)**…you! So get on your knees and dive into Scripture. You're going to need it. Thank you for joining us for this battle, straight from the desert of Judea. Goodbye!

Questions

- Share a time when you have been tempted.
- What did Jesus do to fight the temptations?
- What can you do to fight the devil's temptations?

Story Extension Ideas

- Fight temptation with the Word of God. Have each child fashion a sword out of poster board and read Ephesians 6:10-19. Have each child write temptations they are prey to on one side of the sword. On the other side, they can write a verse, such as Hebrews 4:15-16, to help them battle temptation.
- Look up Scriptures on temptation, such as Matthew 6:13, 1 Corinthians 10:12-13, and James 1:12-17. Play The Pull of Temptation by marking a line on the floor and having several children stand on one side of the line with the rest of the class on the other. The smaller group will try to pull kids across the line. Children may help keep each other from crossing the "sin" line.

Other Story Possibilities

- You can tell many Bible stories with cue cards. Let the class help you create your own. Adam and Eve were the first to fall victim to temptation. You can use the same cue cards for this story, found in Genesis 3.
- Joshua 6–7 tells the story of Jericho's fall and the temptation Achan succumbed to in regard to the devoted things. Retell it from Achan's point of view.

K-3

Eye (I) Witness

Is it magic or a miracle? That's what children will ask when you turn water into "wine" before their very eyes. Let them experience the wonder the disciples felt as they witnessed a miracle. The children will participate in the joy of the wedding and the awe at Jesus. Who was this man Jesus who could turn water into wine and a band of scruffy fisherman into eyewitnesses to the power of God?

The Story

Water Into Wine, John 2:1-11

The Point

Jesus is God.

The Materials

Ceramic or stone vase, one package of red powdered drink mix, one cup of sugar, water in a pitcher, plastic flowers, long white gown, veil, flower garland, dress-up clothes (headdresses, tunics, necklaces, and bracelets), music, and tape recorder. Optional: a wedding cake or other fancy food

Preparation

Find some joyous music and pop it into the tape recorder. For even greater effect, find some Hebrew music to make it more realistic. Before the children arrive, wash out and dry a ceramic or stone pot or vase. Mix a package of red powdered drink mix and a cup of sugar. Pour it into the bottom of the vase. Put the plastic flowers on top, and place the vase on a shelf.

Directions

Gather the materials and prepare for a celebration. You may even want to hang some streamers to make the room look festive. If time allows, let the kids throw a handful of rice at the bride and groom.

Let's Begin

A wedding! What a happy day! Jesus, his disciples, and his mother, Mary, were invited. It seemed like the whole town of Cana turned out for the celebration. The guests prepared for the wedding by wearing their fanciest clothes. *(Let all the kids get dressed up. Choose a bride and groom.)* The bride wore a long, white gown that was beautifully embroidered. She wore lots of jewels and covered herself with a veil. A garland of flowers was placed on her head and on the groom's as well.

The groom left his home with his friends to go to the house of his bride's parents. The wedding party went along, with musicians and singers accompanying them. *(Have the class go to one side of the room and walk with the group to the bride's "home." Turn on the music.)*

The bridegroom received his bride with joy, and they went back to his house to have the party. *(The group goes back to the groom's "house.")* Jesus, his disciples, Mary, and all the others enjoyed sharing this special day. Well into the night there was laughter, dancing, music, singing, and wine—plenty of wine. *(Show the children how to do a Hebrew-style wedding dance. The bride and groom hold hands in the middle, and the class encircles them. They put their hands on each other's shoulders and dance in a circle around them.)*

Weddings back then lasted for at least a week! That's a lot of meals to have to serve to a lot of people—and a lot of wine to share.

After three days, Mary came up to Jesus. She whispered in his ear, "Jesus, there's a little problem. It's rather embarrassing for the bride and groom. The wine is gone." *(Stop the music.)*

Jesus said, "Dear woman, why are you telling me this? It is not yet my time."

Did that stop Mary? No. She went right up to the servants and said, "Do whatever Jesus tells you."

Nearby stood six huge stone water pots. They probably looked something like this pot here. *(Bring over the vase with the flowers in it. Take out the flowers, but don't let the kids see what's inside. If you have them sit on the floor and look up at you working on the table, they won't see.)* Jesus said to the servants, "Fill the jars with water."

Surely some of the servants thought, Why are we pouring water in here? They need wine, not water. But the servants poured jar after jar of water into the empty stone pots. *(Pour the water from the pitcher into the vase, making sure that all the children see that it is water you are pouring in. Swirl it around a bit.)*

Then they poured some out, and it was...*(Pour some into a cup with all the children watching.)*...WHAT? This isn't water. It's...*(Taste it.)*...wine! Delicious, wet, fruity wine! They brought it to the master of ceremonies who tasted it and said, "Why did you save the best for the last? This was the best wine he had ever tasted. *(Start music and pour the kids a drink. Make sure they know it's not really wine and that it was a trick done with drink mix in the pot.)*

"It's a miracle! A miracle!" the people cried. Perhaps they all pushed and shoved to get a taste. But Jesus had made plenty of wine for everyone. Now there was more reason to celebrate. You never know what will happen when you invite Jesus into your life or party!

This was the first of Jesus' miracles. It showed his power and glory. For only God can make something out of nothing and wine out of plain old everyday water. And his disciples believed in him. *(Have the wedding cake and continue the party.)*

Questions

- How did you feel when you saw that the water had changed?
- How do you think the people at the wedding party felt when Jesus made wine from water?
- How are these two changes different?
- What does this show about who Jesus is?
- What can Jesus do in your life?

Story Extension Ideas

- Show the children how to do this simple trick. Have them write the following poem on a paper and use the paper for the trick. Lay a penny in the middle of a piece of paper. Fold the paper into thirds lengthwise. Let the penny secretly slip onto your lap. Then fold it in thirds horizontally. Tap it and open. No penny! Let the kids try.

  Jesus did no magic, but the people were awed.
  Jesus did miracles to show us he's God.
  When he changed the water into wine,
  The light of Jesus began to shine.

- Have the kids make this craft. Each child gets two plastic tumblers. One is painted red on the outside. On the bottom of this cup, they write with a permanent marker, "in him." On the outside of the other cup, the kids write, "Jesus showed his glory, and his disciples put their faith…" (John 2:11). They fill this second cup with water. As the kids say their full verse, they put the cup of water into the cup of "wine."

Other Story Possibilities

- Let the kids become an Eye (I) Witness to the miraculous multiplication of the fish and loaves in Mark 8. In a basket, hide a lot of fish-shaped crackers and small rolls. Cover it with a cloth napkin. Put a few fish-shaped crackers and seven rolls on top of the napkin. As you tell the story, reach under the napkin to produce quantities of fish and bread.
- The death in the pot story can be seen and tasted. Read 2 Kings 4:38-41. Add cranberries to a pot of stew, and let the kids taste it. Pretend you are Elisha tossing flour in the stew. Really it will be sugar, giving a sour tale a sweet ending.

4-5

Objective Detective

Transform your students into collective detectives, gathering clues and interviewing witnesses. The kids will discover evidence hiding at the scene of the "crime," investigate fingerprints, and test alibis. Pooling their data at headquarters, the children will sleuth for the truth to decide if suspect Simon (alias Peter) is a disciple of Jesus Christ. If you were charged with being a Christian, is there enough evidence to convict you?

The Story

The Life of Peter, Luke 5:1-11, and 1 Peter 1

The Point

We need to live our lives for Christ.

The Materials

Five actors, photocopies of the handout titled "Suspect Simon" (pp. 94-95), ink pad, red paint or marker, yellow streamers, NIV Bible, concordance, and a can of tuna. Clues to hide: sword made of poster board, wet sandals in Peter's size, a receipt reading "4,000 denarii for sale of fish" (with a date two years earlier), a feather, a rock, and a piece of paper with words smudged out. (The only words that show are "Pete, an ap........strangers in the world...") Optional: a light to shine on the suspect, a detective's raincoat, hat, cell phone, and a magnifying glass.

Preparation

Make a sword out of poster board. Use an ink pad to put Peter's fingerprints on the sword handle and red paint or marker to show some blood on the tip. Get five adults or youths to read their scripts. Try to practice once before class. Hide the clues in another room or area, and rope the "crime scene" with streamers twisted around chairs.

Directions

Follow the script. Once the kids have found the clues, they can sit down and watch the rest of the skit. Wanda Witness and Malchus start inside the crime scene.

Let's Begin

See the handout on pages 94-95.

SUSPECT SIMON

Detective Circumspective (alias DC): *(Answering cell phone)* Yeah. DC here. What? No way. Sounds like you got a real nut case on your hands. I'll get my crew and be at headquarters ASAP. First, we'll gather the data. Ten-four. Over. *(Puts away phone. Turns to class.)* Folks, we've got a possible psychopathic lunatic being held at the station. Claims to be a follower of Jesus Christ. Let's search the scene of the crime for evidence. But be careful. If this guy is a Christian, there could be others like him who are armed and dangerous.

(Go to another room where the clues have been hidden and the room is roped off with yellow crime scene tape. The kids can search for and pick up the clues.)

DC: OK. Let's get down to headquarters. Bring in those two suspects for questioning.

(Go back to the room, and have children lay out the evidence on the table. Peter is sitting at a table with a light glaring into his face. Kids sit down to watch.)

DC: Officer Do Do, here are the clues from the crime scene. We also found two witnesses.

Officer Do Do (alias ODD): Here's the suspect—says his name is Simon.

Malchus: His name is Peter. I heard Jesus call him that after he cut my ear off.

DC: So what is it, Peter or Simon? I never trust people with an alias, except me of course.

(If kids know any information about Peter's name and calling, let them share it now.)

Peter: My name was Simon, but Jesus renamed me Peter. We were all gathered around the fire one night. Jesus asked us, "Who do the people say I am?" We replied, "Some say John the Baptist; others say Elijah; and still others say one of the prophets." Jesus asked me, "What about you, who do you say I am?" I said, "You are the Christ, the Son of the living God." Jesus said I was blessed. He renamed me "Peter," which means "rock."

DC: Okaaay. We'll call you Peter until the formal investigation before the grand jury.

ODD: Hey, boss, looks like he could be telling the truth. A rock was found at the scene.

DC: Tag it as Exhibit #1.

ODD: What about those mysterious wet sandals?

DC: What's so strange about wet sandals for a fisherman?

ODD: It's how he says they got wet that's strange. Says he actually walked on the water with Jesus—like we'd believe that.

(If kids know any information about Peter walking on water, let them share it now.)

DC: Give it to us straight, mister.

Peter: It's true—wild, but true. We were in our boat one night when a storm arose. During the fourth watch of the night, we saw this eerie shape approaching our boat. We all screamed, thinking it was a ghost. But it was Jesus. He was really walking on the water. I called out to him, "Lord, if it's you, tell me to come to you on the water." He told me to come to him. So I stepped out of the boat and walked on the water with Jesus. I did great while I kept my eyes on him. But when I looked at the storm around me, I got afraid and started to sink. He reached out his hand and rescued me.

DC: A likely story.

ODD: Doesn't sound too likely to me.

DC: Check the foot size to see if they really are his sandals, and then tag them as Exhibit #2. What about this? *(Picks up receipt.)* This receipt says you got 4,000 denarii for one day's catch. Now come on, there aren't even that many fish in the Sea of Galilee.

ODD: *(Picking up the receipt)* It must be a fraud.

(If kids know any information about the miraculous catch of fish, let them share it now.)

Peter: It's true, I tell you. We were discouraged because we had fished all night without getting even one bite. When we were pulling our boats to shore, Jesus asked us to try once more. Just to humor him, we did it. We pulled in so many fish that our nets started to break. I called another boat to help. Even when we had divided up the fish, the boats started to sink! I'd been a fisherman my whole life and had never seen anything like it!

ODD: There **was** an overpowering fish smell at the scene of the crime.

DC: *(Holding up other paper and inspecting it with the magnifying glass)* Hmmm. Says here, "Peter, an ap... strangers in the world..." What could this mean?

ODD: "Peter, an ap..." Peter, an apple collector? An ape?

(Let the kids guess what "ap" could mean.)

DC: What about this part..."strangers in the world?"

ODD: I'll say this is strange and getting stranger.

DC: The guys in Forensics suggested we use one of these to figure it out.

(Hand a concordance to one of the kids. Show them how to look up the word "strangers" alphabetically. Let them look up various verses in their NIV Bibles that have the word "strangers" in it and conclude that the real verse is 1 Peter 1:1.)

ODD: Aha, so here we have proof. He admits in writing to being an apostle of Jesus Christ. Tag that as Exhibit #3.

DC: Have him write out the verse for handwriting analysis purposes.

ODD: Smooth thinking.

DC: So now you're telling me this guy is also a writer of the Bible?

ODD: Looks like we've got proof positive. What about the weapon we found?

DC: *(Hands him the sword. They match Peter's fingerprints to the ones on the sword.)* So we've identified him as the owner of the weapon.

Malchus: I could have told you that. That guy chopped off my ear last night!

DC: (*Inspecting his ear*) Look, Malchus, you may be a servant to the high priest, but you are obviously a pathological liar.

ODD: Look, buddy, we weren't born yesterday. We can see you've got two ears.

Malchus: I'm telling you, that guy cut my ear clean off! I saw it lying on the ground. The weird thing is that Jesus touched the bloody spot on my head and a new ear appeared.

DC: Take the sword to the crime lab, and get a sample of his blood. We may even need to check the DNA. This is getting weirder.

Servant Girl: Peter or Simon or whoever he is—he is a liar. He told me three times last night that he didn't know Jesus Christ. But I'm no fool. You can tell from his accent—he's a Galilean like Jesus.

DC: OK, Peter, why on earth are you claiming to be a Christian today when you denied even knowing Jesus last night?

Peter: Well, I...

Servant Girl: If you're not man enough to say it, I will. Right after he tells me that he doesn't know Jesus, a rooster crows. Jesus happens to walk by just then, all handcuffed and surrounded by guards. But Jesus looks right at Peter, and Peter looks right at him. Next thing I know, this big, grown man here runs away from our fire, bawling like a baby. I don't get any of it.

Peter: What she says is true. I'm ashamed to admit it, but I denied Jesus. I won't do it again. (*Stands up.*) Jesus is the Christ, the Son of the living God, and the best friend a person ever had. I'll not deny him again, even if I get the death penalty!

DC: We need some witnesses to check out his story.

ODD: Negative, sir. All the other apostles have disappeared without a trace. We did, however, find this. (*Hands him the feather.*) It belongs to a rooster.

DC: So what is it, Simon Peter? Are you fisherman, soldier, author, or lunatic?

Peter: I'm an apostle of Jesus Christ, by the will of God.

DC: Okay, buddy, I believe you. Now I want to find out about this Jesus.

ODD: Boss, looks like we've got the evidence, the motive, and the witnesses. I'd say he's telling the truth. The question is what about you? *(Points to the audience.)* Is there enough evidence to convict you of being a follower of Jesus Christ?

Questions

- How did Peter feel about denying Jesus?
- Has there ever been a time when you have denied Christ?
- What does your life look like to nonbelievers? Is there evidence of your Christianity?

Story Extension Ideas

- Make a lie detector test (a "shakeometer"), and have the kids interrogate Peter. He holds a pencil on two fingers while the kids question him. If the pencil shakes, it proves he's lying.
- Make a "Wanted" poster of each child in your class. Take a picture of each child holding a card in front of his or her chest, with Romans 1:16 written on it. Take profile shots, too. Let kids fill in the following information on their posters: description, last seen at, crime wanted for: being a follower of Jesus Christ.

Other Story Possibilities

- Use clues to discover Bible truths from other Bible stories. Use a similar theme from Acts to accuse Paul. Use eyewitnesses and evidence such as snakebites on the arm, his letters, or a letter from the Sanhedrin securing permission to capture Christians.
- Decide whether Benjamin is guilty of first-degree burglary and whether Joseph will forgive him (Genesis 43–45). Spray paint a goblet silver, and hide it in a grain sack. Use money, spices, honey, and nuts as other clues.

K-3

Shine the Shadows

Stories are told through emotions etched on the human face. Cut plastic foam plates into simple faces, and then shine a flashlight through the plates. The images are projected onto the wall as you tell the story. Watch your children's faces express wonder and joy while you tell the tale of the world's best fisherman.

The Story

Peter's Big Catch, Luke 5:1-11

The Point

Following Jesus may mean giving up something in our lives.

The Materials

Plastic foam plates (at least seven, preferably nineteen), a pen or permanent marker, knife, and flashlight

Preparation

According to the list below, use a pen or permanent marker to draw one face by hand onto each plate. Use a sharp knife to cut the features. Number the faces. Make sure the room you use can be fully darkened and has a blank wall on which you can project the images. Plates should have the following expressions: frown, talking, closed eyes, sad smile, surprise, and big smile.

Directions

Stack the plates in the order they will be used in the story. You may want to cut extra plates according to the following numbers so you won't need to fumble about in the dark: frown (3), talking (4), closed eyes (2), sad, (3), smile (1), surprise (3), big smile (3). Hold the flashlight and the plates yourself, or ask a helper to hold up the plates while you tell the story. Give any children who may be afraid of the dark an opportunity to sit near you.

Let's Begin

(Plate 1: Frown) Peter grumbled as he watched the sunset. "Now we'll never see the fish when we finally do catch them."

(Plate 2: Talking) "Don't worry, Peter," John said. "Soon the moon will come out, and we can fish by moonlight."

As their little boat bobbed up and down on the Sea of Galilee, Peter and his friends tried all night to catch some fish. The moon played Hide-and-Seek behind clouds. In the dark, the sea calmed. It seemed to turn into a still mirror, without a ripple or the splash of a leaping fish.

(Plate 3: Closed eyes) John's eyelids struggled to stay open. You could see Peter yawn. You could see James pulling seaweed out of the net.

(Plate 4: Sad) All night long, the men threw the dripping nets overboard and then hauled them in—empty. All night long, the men ran their fingers over the strings, hoping they'd feel something scaly and slippery. All night long, the men prayed for some fish so they could sell them. They needed the money. But they caught nothing.

(Plate 5: Frown) Finally, as the sun crept into the sky, Peter growled, "What a waste of time! Let's forget this and go home for a nap."

(Plate 6: Closed eyes) He stood up and stretched, rocking the boat. James pulled on a rope, trimming the sail to catch the light morning breeze. Their boat skimmed swiftly across the water. As the men climbed out of the boat and were washing their nets, they noticed a crowd gathering nearby.

(Plate 7: Talking) "What are all those people doing out this early?" John asked.

"I hope they're not waiting to buy our fish. We haven't any to sell," James said.

Peter leaned over the bow where he was storing the ropes, staring intently at the shore. "It's Jesus!"

(Plate 8: Smile) The crowd pushed closer and closer to Jesus, hoping to catch every word that he spoke. Soon Jesus' sandals were getting wet, he was so close to the shore.

"Peter," Jesus said, "Can I please use your boat to talk to the crowd?"

(Plate 9: Talking) "Yes, of course, Master." Peter untied the rope and walked the boat out a bit into shallow water. Then Jesus sat down and spoke the words of God to the people. They swallowed his words like breakfast.

When he finished speaking, Jesus said to Peter, "Peter, put your boat out into deep water, and let down the nets for a catch."

(Plate 10: Surprise) Peter stopped. His eyebrows shot up. He looked at John. He looked at James. James shrugged his shoulders. They seemed to be silently saying to each other, "Nobody goes fishing this late in the day."

(Plate 11: Sad) "Master," Peter said with a big sigh, "we've worked hard all night and haven't caught anything. But because you say so, I will let down the nets."

Jesus settled into the boat. Peter threw the ropes on board. Sloshing through water up to his waist, he pushed off and jumped aboard. Peter, James, John, and Jesus sailed out a short way.

(Plate 12: Talking) "OK," Peter said, "let down the net." They lowered the nets overboard and waited a few minutes.

"Haul them in," Peter commanded. James and John tried to pull the net in.

"This net must be snagged on something below," James said.

"Pull a little harder," said John.

(Plate 13: Frown) Peter helped them pull until their muscles hurt. The boat tipped. The water started to churn. What did they see as they pulled the net to the surface? Their net was full of hundreds of slippery, sloshy, silvery, flippy, floppy fish!

(Plate 14: Surprise) Their eyes nearly popped out. Peter's mouth opened wide and then turned into a big smile.

(Plate 15: Big smile) James and John shouted with joy. In all their years of fishing, they

had never seen anything like it.

As they tried to haul the fish onto their boat, the nets started to rip. Peter called to some other fisherman in another boat,

(Plate 16: Surprise) "Come help us! We've got more fish than you've ever seen."

(Plate 17: Big smile) Our boat can't even handle them!" he said with a laugh.

The other fishermen came to help. They filled their boat, too. Soon both boats were so full of twisting, slippery fish that the boats actually started to sink!

Now some of the other fishermen may have been thinking about how much money they'd make from the huge catch of fish. Not Peter.

(Plate 18: Sad) Peter fell at Jesus' knees right into a pile of fish. He said, "Go away from me, Lord, I am a sinful man." You see, Peter and all his friends realized Jesus was God's son.

(Plate 19: Big smile) Jesus smiled at Peter and said, "Don't be afraid, my friend: From now on you will catch men."

So the men pulled their boats up onto the shore. They left their fish. They left their nets. They left their boats. And they followed Jesus—for the rest of their lives. The fishers of fish became fishers of men, pulling people into Jesus' open arms.

Questions

- How do you think Peter felt leaving his boat, his job, and his way of life to follow Jesus?
- Do you think he was ever sorry he chose to follow Jesus?
- Is there anything in your life you might need to "leave behind" to follow Jesus?

Story Extension Ideas

- Catch some fish. Let the children cut some fish out of construction paper and color them. Attach paper clips to the fish. Fashion a fishing pole from a stick, some string, and a magnet. On the flip side of the fish, have the children write the name of a person who needs to be "caught" for Jesus. As the children catch the fish, have them pray for the person whose name is written on each one.
- Use the plate faces as stencils. Have the children trace the plate faces onto paper to make their own storybooks. Let them practice retelling the story to one another before they share it with others.

Other Story Possibilities

You can use the same faces to tell almost any Biblical tale.

- The two travelers on the road to Emmaus in Luke 24:13-35. will express surprise that the living Son of God had been in their midst and they had failed to recognize him.
- Job experienced every human emotion from agony to joy. Use the plates to tell his tale of woe to worship.

K-5

Rap Song Clap-Along

A rowdy rap song with a pulsating beat can pull the audience in to join and clap. The beauty of rap songs is that the "singer" doesn't need to be able to sing, and a good beat will make up for even beginning writing skills.

The Story

Peter's Watery Walk, Matthew 14:22-33

The Point

You can do all things through Christ.

The Materials

A Bible-times outfit for Peter, drums (optional), and a boat: To make a simple boat, draw some horizontal lines on a large box and bend the ends in for a curved bow. Make a simple mast by sticking a broom into a bucket filled with rocks. From the top of the broom handle, secure an old white sheet, and tape it to the sides of the boat. Make sure the sides of the boat are low enough for Peter to step over. It doesn't have to be fancy for the audience to understand it's supposed to be a boat.

Preparation

Practice the script several times to make sure you get a good rhythm. Dress up in a Bible-times outfit, and if you'd like, you can add drums and lighting to present a unique account of Peter's plunge of faith. Once you see what a hit this rap song is, have older students write one of their own.

Directions

Add hand motions to the song. For example, when it says, "Jesus Christ can walk on any wave...," point right at the audience. Assign someone else the role of getting the audience into the right clapping rhythm. This rap song is better with a lively audience.

Let's Begin

(Start out in the boat.)
Hey, my name is Peter, and I got a song.
So listen up, cause it won't take long.
This story is as real as me and you.
It's right there in the Bible, so you know it's true.

I am one of the twelve disciples.
That's how my name got in the Bible.
I followed Jesus wherever he went.
That's how I got into this predicament.
We were out in the boat, a-sailin' on the sea.
All of the other disciples and me.
Well, the wind grew strong, and the waves splashed high.
I wanted my Jesus to be nearby.
But I knew that Jesus was up in the hills,
Prayin' to God to know his will.
That's why, deep in the middle of this stormy night,
We saw a sight that gave us a bad FRIGHT!
(Silence.)
Through the wind
And the waves
Through the darkness, too,
A creepy shape
Was passing through.
My throat went dry;
I started to shake.
What could that be
Walkin' on the lake?
"It's a ghost," a disciple screamed.
That figure out there was not a dream!
It came closer...
And closer...
And closer by.
We were all so scared that we wanted to die.
Then a voice came rollin' across the waves,
(Deep voice) "It is I...Do not be afraid!"
What? That's JESUS out strollin' on the sea,
Just a walkin' footloose and fancy-free.
Why, I could hardly believe my eyes.
Everything with Jesus is big surprise.
When I decided to follow Christ,
I also decided to pay the price.
I truly wanted to walk with him,
But the truth of the matter is
I CAN'T SWIM!

Though I've been in boats my whole life long,
INSIDE the boat is where I belong.
So I yelled, "Lord, if it's really you,
Help me to walk on the water, too."
"Come to me," was his answer, like it always is.
Now I'm gonna show that I'm truly his.
One foot over—two feet—*(Climb out of boat.)* WOW!
I'm walking on the water, and I don't know how!
Look at me! I'm really walkin' on the sea!
I can do all things through Christ, who strengthens me.
Look at me out here a-splashin' with the fish—
Being with Jesus is my only wish.
This is fun, this is cool; it's wild and wet.
But then I looked down, and I started to sweat.
It's DEEP down there, and I can't swim.
I looked at the boat, and I wanted in.
Just then, I started to sink and drown.
I was swallowin' water and goin' down.
"Lord, save me," I cried.
To tell the truth, I was petrified.
Jesus reached out his hand, and he rescued me.
His sad eyes asked, "Why didn't you believe?"
We got into the boat, and the wind stopped blowin',
But that didn't stop us all from knowin'
"Truly you are the Son of God."
We stared at Jesus, and we oohed and aahed.
Jesus Christ can conquer any wave.
He came to earth to heal and save.
So get out of your boat, and follow the Lord.
Peace and heaven will be your reward.
I hope you learn what I did that day.
Come on with me, and let's all say:
I can do all things, even walk on the sea.
I can do all things through Christ who strengthens me.
(Repeat last two lines several times with the whole group.)

Questions

- How did Peter feel when he stepped out of the boat?
- Tell about a time in your life when you had to do something you didn't think you could do.
- How can you let Jesus help you when you need to do hard things?

Story Extensions

- Write on one sheet of paper the word "friends" and on another the word "money." Say: **Jesus wants us to get out of our comfort zones and follow him. We all have boats that we'd rather not get out of. Let's call this boat "friends."** *(Label the boat "friends," and call together a few kids and have them stand in the boat.)* **Jesus may be calling you to get out of the crowd and to be a friend to a child who has no friends. Will you get out of the boat, leave your friends, to follow the Lord? Now, let's call this boat "money." If Jesus asks you to get out of your boat,** *(Give some of your money up.)* **are you willing to? What other "boats" are you sometimes called out of?**
- Ask the children each to write on a piece of paper one thing that they are afraid of. Have them each get into the boat, one at a time, with their paper. They can share aloud their fear or read it silently. Have another child pose as Jesus and help them out of the boat saying, "Take courage! It is I! Don't be afraid" (Matthew 14:27).

Other Story Possibilities

- Wouldn't you love to hear a psalm put to rap? Try it with your older students. See Psalm 148 for starters. Add whatever lines you need to make it work. For example, the first two lines in Psalm 148 could read, "Praise the Lord from the heavens, praise him from above. Praise the Lord from heaven, he fills us up with his love."
- Arch Books, published by Concordia Publishing in St. Louis, Missouri, are picture books of Bible stories that are written in verse. Let the kids break into teams to adapt and practice portions of the book and present the whole story to the class for a makeshift rap song.

K-5

Monologue Mystique

A monologue can mesmerize all ages and sizes of audiences unlike few other techniques. Monologues offer a rare glimpse into another era and another's emotions. This heart-rending story of a leper describes life in a leper colony and allows the children to empathize with this man's horror. The children will experience his healing at the hand the living Son of God.

The Story

The Thankful Leper, Luke 17:11-19

The Point

It is important to thank God.

The Materials

A battery-powered lantern, an old sheet to serve as a tunic, another sheet to cover the head, rags, white face cream, any red makeup, a wet washcloth, and baby powder

Preparation

Practice the script several times. Dress as a leper. Hide a wet washcloth near the lantern. You can edit the script according to the age of your audience.

Directions

To dress as a leper, dab on the white face cream and red makeup. Put dots all over your face and arms. Next, put some baby powder in your hair. All of this washes up easily. Put a sheet over your head, and bind up a leg and a hand with rags. When it's time to make your appearance, curl one hand under the sheet. This will be your "decayed" hand. When the kids are quiet and the lights low, have someone turn on the lantern. Start to thump, thump, thump your way to the lantern, dragging along your "decaying" leg. Use a raspy voice to tell them this moving story.

Let's Begin

Hello, children. I am glad that you have come to hear my story, but please, don't touch me! I have a dreadful disease called leprosy. It is very contagious. That means that if you touch me, you could also get this dreaded disease. I wouldn't wish this awful disease upon even my worst enemy.

Listen well and learn. I lived a very long

time ago in the days of Jesus. One day before I got sick, I woke up and tried to stand up. I couldn't feel anything in my right foot. Falling back down, I shook and shook my leg. Still I felt nothing, as though it wasn't there. Then I got scared. You see, numbness is one of the first signs of leprosy. I ran to the pond outside. "Please, oh, please," I prayed as I ran to see my reflection in the water. "Please don't let me have any white spots." I peered over the edge of the water. Oh no! Big, round, white spots were all over my forehead. I had leprosy!

I raced back to my house and slammed the door. I didn't want anyone to know. Soon, the white spots had spread all over my body. *(Throw back your head and scratch yourself.)* Then my hair turned white. *(Take the sheet off your head.)* My hair will start falling out in big clumps.

I couldn't hide the leprosy any longer. I looked like a lion with my eyebrows, forehead, and ears all scabby and white. To obey the law, I went to see the priest in my town. We have a law here that says lepers must mess up their hair and rip their clothes. As we walk, we must call out in a loud voice, "Unclean, unclean!" People screamed and ran in terror from me. It was so embarrassing. *(Hang your head.)* I felt just like a m-m-monster. You see nobody wants to get leprosy—do you? *(Point your finger closely at the children, and watch them jump back.)*

The priest told me that I had to go live in the leper camp with all the other lepers. I had to say goodbye to my family. *(Rub your eyes.)* I miss them. I hate this leper colony. It smells like putrid flesh. All day and night I hear moans of lepers begging God to either cure them or kill them. Sometimes the other lepers shriek in fear. The flies swarm around my oozing wounds. The worst part is watching the other lepers and knowing that I could end up like them, too. They look like skeletons because the leprosy has eaten away their eyes and noses. You find teeth on the ground, and you see lepers' gums curled up. When they try to talk, they just make animal-like gurgling sounds. The leprosy has already started to attack my throat. That's why I sound like this.

(Hold up a gnarled fist.) See what's left of my hand? After I got to the leper colony, my fingernails started to loosen and peel off. My fingers started to shrivel, and then my fingers started to disappear. Joint by joint. *(Hold up your hand and slowly curl it into a fist, then cover it with the sheet.)* Soon, I'll lose my eyesight.

(Leave a few moments of silence.) One day I was with nine other lepers near the gate of the city. We begged for food from people passing by. One leper jumped up and growled, "Look, it's Jesus of Nazareth." We all crowded around to peer through the gate.

"I hear that Jesus can heal people," I said hopefully.

Another leper said, "Yes, he has healed blind and crippled people, but he won't stop for us. Do you think he wants to get our leprosy?"

"That's right," another leper said. "Besides, look at that crowd around Jesus. Why would he care about some rotting humans like us?"

"Yes, and don't forget, Jesus is a Jew and Jews hate us Samaritans, remember?"

But I was desperate. I started to call out loud, "Jesus, Master, have pity on us!"

Soon the other nine lepers joined me. In our raspy, screeching voices we cried louder and louder, "Jesus, Master, have pity on us!"

(Pause.) Jesus stopped. He looked at us.

"He-he is coming!" I yelled.

Jesus did come to us and simply said, "Go show yourselves to the priests."

Silently, wondering, we walked away from him toward the temple. As I walked, dragging my decaying leg, all of a sudden, I felt STRONG. *(Stand up straight, and take the bandages off your leg.)* Listen, my voice—it's normal again! My skin—it doesn't itch anymore. My hand. My hand is healed! *(Uncurl your fingers.)* And all those horrid white spots are...*(Use a wet washcloth to wipe off makeup.)*...GONE! I'm healed. I'm healed! *(Jump up and down.)*

All ten of us lepers were cured. We leaped for joy and hugged one another. *(Hug a child or two.)* My friends ran home to tell their families about the miracle. But not me. I ran back to Jesus, praising God in a loud, healthy voice. I threw myself at Jesus' feet *(Fall on your knees.)* and kissed him crying, "Thank you. Thank you, Jesus."

Jesus looked down at me with gentle, sad eyes and asked, "Were not ten lepers healed? Where are the other nine?"

I was glad I went back to Jesus. And so, my young friends, Jesus is waiting for you, too. Remember to thank him for all he has done for you.

Questions

- How did you feel when the leper described life in the leper colony?
- How did you feel when the leper was healed?
- Tell about a time that God did something very special for you.
- How can you remember to say thank you to Jesus for the wonderful things he does in your life?

Story Extensions

- Discuss with the children times when God has done something special in their lives. Let them write and decorate thank-you notes to God.
- Take the children to a nursing home to visit those people who are restricted to life in an institution. Ask the director if you can visit with the people who have no family to visit them. You can have the children make cards before they go and learn several songs to share. Compassion is a key character quality of God, and we need to instill it in our kids.

Other Story Possibilities

Older students can learn how to research Biblical characters and present their own monologues.

- Pilate's wife dreamed of Jesus. What was her dream about? How did she try to convince her husband to let Jesus go free in Matthew 27? How did she feel when Jesus was condemned?
- Wouldn't you love to have been a mouse in the house of Michal and David when David escaped through a window? How was Michal torn between her loyalty to her father and her husband? See 1 Samuel 18 and 19.

K-5

Play Day

To re-enact a Bible story is to remember it forever. When a child becomes the trodden traveler, he moves beyond the cognitive into the realm of emotional expression, thus imprinting indelibly into his memory the character's encounters. Writing their own scripts allows children to explore the feelings and attitudes of the people whom Jesus touched and understand the "why" beyond the "what" that Scripture lays before us. This skit will teach children to dive into their own dramas (without trauma).

The Story

The Good Samaritan, Luke 10:25-37

The Point

Make time for God and others.

The Materials

Bible-time outfits (or modern-day outfits), sticks, a sign labeled "The Come In Inn" or any name of your choosing, cloth for bandages, oil, two silver coins. Optional: donkey. (Make one by drawing a picture of a donkey and attach it to a rolling chair.)

Preparations

Make photocopies of the handout titled "Who Is My Neighbor" (pp. 108-109) for each person in the class. You can create extra parts in the play by breaking up the narrator's speaking parts into Narrator #1, Narrator #2, and so on. For smaller classes, you can combine roles. Ask for volunteers for the parts listed below. If you have a child who doesn't like to read, assign him to be the props captain. Have each person highlight his or her lines before the play begins. Have them each dress and prepare the props.

Directions

Have the kids read their parts and act them out as the play progresses. Then think about taking your show on the road. Ask the class if they'd like to memorize their parts and entertain a younger class.

Let's Begin

See the handout on pages 108-109.

WHO IS MY NEIGHBOR?

CAST:
Narrator, Expert in the law, Jesus, Traveler, Robber(s), Priest, Levite, Samaritan, Innkeeper

Narrator: One day Jesus was teaching the crowds of people. Most people came to learn from Jesus and love him more. But some people came to see if they could trick Jesus. One man thought he would give Jesus a really tough question. This man had studied the holy Scriptures for years. He loved the Lord his God with all of his mind but not with his heart and his soul. He stood up and asked Jesus…

Expert: Teacher, what must I do to have eternal life? How can I live forever in heaven?

Jesus: What is written in the Bible? How do you read it?

Expert: Love the Lord your God with all your heart and with all your strength and with all your soul and with all your mind. And love your neighbor as yourself.

Jesus: Right! Do this and you will live.

Expert: And just what do you mean by that? I live in a busy city with people all around me. WHO is my neighbor?

Jesus: I thought you'd never ask. I'll answer with a story.

Narrator: This is the story Jesus told. A traveler, a Jewish man, was going from Jerusalem to Jericho. He was walking along, *(Whistle.)* minding his own business, when suddenly two robbers jumped out from behind a rock.

Robber 1: Give me all your money!

Traveler: But I haven't got any.

Robber 1: Let's get 'im.

Robber 2: Uh-uh. OK, boss.

Narrator: The robbers stripped the man of his clothes. They beat the man until he crumbled to the ground.

Traveler: Aahh.

Robber 1: Uh-oh, boss. I tink we killed da guy. Gulp.

Robber 2: Quick, let's get out of here.

Narrator: So the poor man lay there on the side of the road. He wasn't dead, but he was knocked out and lay there in a heap, bleeding and in need of help. The hot sun beat down on him. He couldn't even drag himself to the shade. The traveler could feel footsteps on the ground and thought, Here comes someone to help me. A priest was walking by. He walked over to the lump in the road to see what it was. He kicked it.

Traveler: Aahh!

Priest: *(Shrieking)* Yahh, it's alive—I mean, he's alive! Will you look at that! Now I got blood on my brand new sandal! What will the people in church think when they see me with blood on my feet? Sorry, buddy, but I just can't preach with blood all over me. I'm sure you understand. I—uh—I hope somebody helps you.

Narrator: And so the priest hurried away. The day wore on and on. The traveler tried to get up but fell down again.

Traveler: Oohh, the pain, heelpp, someone!

Narrator: Along came a Levite. Levites were religious men who took care of the church.

Levite: *(With hands folded and Bible under the arm)* Oh, my. What have we here? I simply don't have time for this sort of thing. My, what a terrible mess. I'll just cross on over to this side of the street. I AM on my way to the temple, and I would certainly hate to be late by getting involved in such a dreadfully sticky situation. Oh dear—well, I know—let me look in my Bible to see what I can do about this. *(He flips* *pages.)* Ah, yes. Here in Luke 10:27 it says to love the Lord your God with all your heart and soul and strength and mind and to love your neighbor as yourself. Well, hmm...I KNOW. At church I can put him on the prayer list! Yes, that's what I'll do. OH, I am so proud of myself for thinking of that. Certainly somebody who has less important things to do than I do will help that man.

Traveler: Please, dear God, please send someone to help me!

Narrator: Along came a third man. Now this man did love the Lord his God with all his heart and soul and strength and mind, and he loved his neighbor as himself. He proved it, too, even though he was a Samaritan. Now, Samaritans and Jews did not like each other. But the Samaritan man didn't even think about that when he saw the poor Jewish man in pain and bleeding.

Samaritan: Oh, let me help you. Here, take a drink, and here, I'll rip up my shirt for you to stop your bleeding. I even have some oil for your wounds.

Traveler: Thank you, kind sir. Are you Jesus?

Samaritan: No, but I know him. We'll find you a good inn so you can rest and recover. I'll let you ride on my own donkey.

Narrator: The good Samaritan walked and let the traveler ride. He took the traveler to a hotel and took care of him the whole day. The next day, when he had to get home, the Samaritan paid two silver coins to the innkeeper.

Samaritan: Here. This is to continue taking care of the traveler until he is better.

Innkeeper: Sir, are you Jesus?

Samaritan: No. I'm not, but I know him.

Narrator: Jesus finished his story and turned to the expert.

Jesus: Now, which of these three men was a neighbor to the traveler?

Expert: The one who helped him.

Jesus: Right! Go and do the same.

Questions

- How do you think the traveler felt when no one would stop to help him?
- How did he feel when the Samaritan DID make time to help him?
- Can you share a time when someone made time for you?
- Who do you think about when we talk about making time for another person? Let's pray right now that we'll be obedient to God and make time for that person God has put in your heart.

Story Extension Ideas

- Have the class make a picture book titled "Loving my Neighbor." Have the kids snap pictures of everyone in the class to put into the book. Add photographs of neighbors and even pictures from magazines. Record ways to love those people.
- Make some cookies and collect canned goods. Go together to a homeless shelter, and interview several of the residents to learn their plight.

Other Story Possibilities

- Almost any Bible story can be told and retold using a play. Keep a few costumes on hand for spontaneous skits. Re-enact the story of Jesus healing the bleeding woman and raising the dead girl to life from Mark 5:21-43.
- King David was dramatic even when his life wasn't in danger. When it was, he really turned on the theatrics. See 1 Samuel 21 for a wild story about a wild man.

K-3

Balloon Cartoons

This approach may even send your audience of any size "soaring." Helium balloons become the canvas for simple line drawings. This particular story compares and contrasts two characters, the rich fool and the poor widow. The fool's earthly treasures come to a loud ending. But the widow's deeds will last forever, symbolized by the balloons floating off to heaven.

The Story

Rich Fool/Poor Widow, Luke 12:16-21 and Mark 12:41-44

The Point

Give our all for Jesus.

The Materials

Four helium balloons, four regular balloons, a permanent marker, two coins, a straight pin, and children to hold the balloons or a way to secure the balloons to a chair

Preparation

Read the story, and practice drawing the pictures on paper several times before presenting the story to the children. Think about where you can tell this story. This story is effective indoors, but can you select a spot where the children can watch the balloons disappear into the sky? Perhaps the children can sit outdoors on a blanket. Keep the straight pin in a pocket. Helium balloons last up to six hours in air conditioning, but may last only thirty minutes in the heat, so plan accordingly. If possible, put two coins into one of the balloons before the helium is injected. Be careful to pick up any broken balloon pieces as they do present a choking hazard.

Directions

Choose four children to stand in front of the group and hold the balloons. Ask them to hold their balloons still so that everyone in the group can see them. Later in the story, after the balloons are popped, choose four more children to hold the other four balloons. Try to draw the pictures as large as possible, being careful not to hide the balloons with your body. Draw the pictures as the story progresses. (If you have someone named Greg in your audience, change the first character's name.)

Let's Begin

Are rich people always rich with God? We'll find out. Jesus told two tales about two very different people with two very different endings to their lives. We find these stories in the Bible in the books of Luke and Mark.

(On Balloon 1 draw a picture of wheat growing.) Greedy Greg strolled through the fields on his farm. He strutted past tall, golden, waving seas of wheat. He squeezed through the vineyard brimming with ripe, purple grapes. He plucked a fat grape and popped it into his mouth. The juice squirted down his beard. "Ahh," he said, "my fields are fantastic! This is the best wheat crop I've ever had. And look at all these grapes I've grown."

Greedy Greg snapped his fingers. Three servants came running to him, "Yes, master," they said. "What can we do for you, sir?"

(On Balloon 2 draw a picture of Greedy Greg scowling.) "These crops are ripe and ready to be harvested. Get going. I want my barns full," Greedy Greg demanded.

"Master, sir," one servant said, "we have a problem, sir. I don't know where to put all the grain. The barns are already overflowing with corn and grain and cattle and..."

(On Balloon 3 draw a picture of Greg smiling or with a light bulb above him indicating getting an idea.) Greg pounded his fist into his hand. "Bigger barns! Now that's the smart thing to do. I'll just tear down my old barns and cram all the grain I possibly can into new, bigger barns. Ha! It's my land, my crops, and my barns—mine, mine, mine. I'll do as I please. Now get going, and start ripping apart my worthless old barns. I'll make plans for huge, fancy, new barns."

(On Balloon 4 draw a picture of a barn.) The servants scurried away. Greg sat down on a hill trying to imagine what his new barns would look like. They would bulge with food. People would come from all over just to stare at these amazing barns. "And I'll take life easy," Greedy Greg said to himself. "I'll have plenty of food for years. I'll give parties. I'll relax. I'll eat steak every night. I'll drink as much wine as I want. I'll..."

Just then a cloud cast a shadow over the hill. At first, Greg thought he heard thunder. Then he realized it was the voice of God, saying, "You fool! This very night your life will be demanded from you. Then who will get what you have prepared for yourself?"

And that is exactly what happened. Greedy Greg died instantly, and *(Pop the four balloons.)* his earthly kingdom vanished too.

(Choose four new children to hold four new balloons.)

(On Balloon 1 draw a picture of a woman with a smile.) In the other story, Jesus told about a wonderful woman who was a widow. We'll call her Wendy.

Wendy's husband had died years before. She had sold everything in her house so she would have money to buy food. Oxen, clothes, fields, and furniture—nothing was left except the garments she wore. She was too old to get a job. And Wendy was hungry. Reaching into a flour jug, she felt around only to get her fingertips dusty. There was not even a cup of flour to make a small loaf of bread.

(On Balloon 2 draw two coins.) Wendy's stomach grumbled. With a sigh, she dragged herself to the corner of the house and started to

claw at the ground. Her nails got brown with dirt, but she didn't care. She dug and dug. There they were—the two coins she had buried years ago. Wendy rubbed them off on her coat. "I've been saving this money for years. Now I really need it," she said. The two coins were worth less than a penny. Wendy folded her fingers around the coins and headed for the marketplace. But before she left, she bowed her head and said a prayer: "Dear Lord, thank you for this money. You have given me life and breath. Now I give back to you everything I have left. You are my love and my life. Amen."

(On Balloon 3 draw a treasure box.) Wendy held her head high as she walked through the busy streets. Did she go to the marketplace to buy a fish or bread? No. Wendy walked to the temple, God's house. She waited in line to go in, hoping no one would hear her stomach growl. My, it's crowded today, Wendy thought.

There was a special visitor that day. His name was Jesus. Jesus sat across from the money box with his disciples, watching the people put their money into the treasure box. One man carried a bag of coins that clattered loudly as they fell into the box. He looked around at the people hoping someone noticed how much money he had put in.

(On Balloon 4 draw a hand dropping two coins in. Use the balloon that has two coins hidden inside.) Jesus sat quietly looking and listening. Then it was Wendy's turn. Wendy covered her face with her veil. She opened her palm and jingle, jingle, *(Shake the balloon.)* gave both coins to God.

Someone did hear that gentle jingle, someone who knew that those were Wendy's last coins. It was Jesus. He smiled at her. Jesus said, "I tell you the truth, this poor widow has put more money into the treasury than all the others. They gave only a little bit of their money. But she gave everything she had."

We don't know how long Wendy lived, but we do know that…*(Have the kids let go of the balloons.)*…Wendy and her love for God will last forever and ever and ever.

Questions

- How did the rich man feel about his wealth?
- How did the widow feel about being poor?
- Tell about something special you have given to Jesus.
- How did you feel when you gave it?
- Think of something else you can do or give to Jesus. Tell a partner about it.

Story Extension Ideas

- Let each child write a prayer of commitment to God. Younger children can draw a picture of what they would like to give to God. Then give each child a bottle of bubbles, and have them blow bubbles into the heavens as they say their prayers.
- Prepare a surprise banquet for Wendy. Have each child bring a food item from home. Make it special with a tablecloth, pretty plates, and a fresh bouquet of flowers. You may want to dress up as Wendy and let the children ask Wendy questions. A simple meal to prepare is sliced turkey, corn-on-the-cob in a crockpot, and rolls.

Other Story Possibilities

● Balloons can become the canvas for many other biblical tales. King Solomon's treasures could chase the wind. See 1 Kings 10–11 and Ecclesiastes. You can use this method to review the kings of Israel and Judah. The "bad" kings' kingdoms can burst, but the "good" kings can float off toward heaven. See 1 and 2 Kings and 2 Chronicles.

● The twelve disciples can all vanish when Jesus is arrested in Matthew 26, except for Peter's balloon. Keep him to creep back to the courtyard. You can rub a regular balloon to create static electricity. This makes a balloon stick to a wall. Talk about sticking by Jesus when we're tempted to run.

K-3

Build the Story

Build this story as you go. Children will actually plant seeds in various types of dirt to tell the parable of the sower. The different types of soil are personalized into children with names and different life situations. Older children will grasp the parallels, and younger children will revel in the hands-on experience.

The Story

The Sower, Seeds, and Soil, Matthew 13:1-23; Mark 4:1-20; and Luke 8:1-15

The Point

We can grow in Jesus.

The Materials

Four plastic foam cups, pen or permanent marker, potting soil, pebbles, spoons, water, your Bible, little twigs or toothpicks, and a healthy potted plant (or artificial flowers)

Preparation

Gather chairs around a table so all the children can see and help. If your group is larger than ten children, you may want to form two groups. Have another helper lead the other group, so that each child can participate in some way in this story. Lay out all the materials, and hide some seeds in your Bible.

Directions

Follow the directions in parentheses. Make sure each child has at least one opportunity to share in this experience. You may want to scatter the pebbles and twigs on the lawn and let the children help you gather them before the story begins.

Let's Begin

Jesus told a story about dirt—good and bad soil. He told us to pretend that the soil is our hearts. This story is in three different books of the Bible, so you know it is very important. I want to have everyone help with this story.

See these four cups? *(Number the cups with permanent marker.)* I need one helper to sprinkle just a little soil in this cup. In Cup 2, I need a little more soil. In Cups 3 and 4, I need a lot of soil. *(Let the children help you put the soil in the cups.)* We are going to see what happens to the seeds we plant in the different kinds of soil.

Jesus loved to tell stories to people, and the people loved to hear his stories. He sometimes taught with parables. A parable is a story using something people know about to teach them something they don't know about. To the fishermen, he taught using fish. To the carpenters, he told stories of building houses. When Jesus taught the farmers, what things do you think he used? Why?

This is the story that Jesus told. One day, a farmer went out to plant his seeds. *(Open your Bible, and let some seeds fall out.)* The farmer took the seeds and scattered them all around. The farmer is like God, and these seeds are the words from his book, the Bible.

(Let a child drop a seed in Cup 1.) God's words went into this child's ears. I'll call him Iggy. Someone told Iggy about Jesus, and he said, "I don't care about all that Bible stuff." When someone invited Iggy to vacation Bible school, he went one day and never went back. Iggy ignored God. *(Show the inside of the cup.)* His heart was just like this soil. There was not enough interest there for God to plant his truth-seed. A big, black bird came. It saw that lonely seed. It snatched the seed and gulped it down. *(Let a child take the seed away.)* The devil is like the bird that grabbed that truth-seed. Satan doesn't want you to put God's word in your heart. Iggy ignored God. He grew up without God. Isn't that sad? *(Draw a sad face on the cup.)*

The next heart *(Pick up Cup 2.)* had a little soil in it. This is like a little girl who went to church and heard about Jesus. I'll call her Joy. Joy was so excited to learn how much Jesus loves her. "Yes!" she said. "I do want Jesus to be my best friend." *(Have a child drop in the seed and another cover it with some soil.)* Like this seed, Joy grew as a Christian. *(Take a flower or stem with leaves from the potted plant. Let a child put it into Cup 2.)* But this soil was very rocky. *(Let the children add the pebbles.)* Rocks make it hard for plants to grow. One day at school, a kid said, "You must be dumb to believe in Jesus." And all the other kids laughed. Joy was heartbroken. She stopped going to church. *(Pluck a leaf.)* She didn't listen to Bible stories, *(Let a child pluck another leaf.)* and she stopped praying to God. *(Let a child pick off the rest of the leaves.)* Joy's pretty little plant just...died. Joy wasn't full of joy anymore. *(Draw a sad face on the cup.)*

The next seed landed in this soil. *(Let a child drop a seed into Cup 3.)* We'll call this child Wanda. This seed grew. *(Let a child put in a stem from the plant.)* Wanda wanted to be a Christian, but she wanted everything else, too. Wanda wanted to have fun, fun, fun and play, play, play. Let's pretend these sticks are all the other things Wanda loved. Wanda wanted to play with her friends instead of going to church. *(Let a child stick in a twig.)* Wanda wanted to read books about horses, but she didn't want to hear many Bible stories. *(Let a child stick in a twig.)* When it was time for dinner, Wanda wanted her food! She didn't want to take time to pray. *(Let a child stick in another twig.)* Pretty soon all those twigs, all the other fun things in life, choked out Wanda's little plant, her love for God. *(Let the children cover the plant with toothpicks or twigs.)* Wanda wanted everything in the world. She got it, but Jesus was forgotten. Wanda ended up sad. *(Draw a sad face on her cup.)*

(Take the last cup, and show them the dirt.) Jose had a heart that was soft and ready to open up and let God in. *(Let a child bury a seed.)* When Jose's dad told him how Jesus could save him, Jose said "yes" to Jesus. Then Jose started to grow. *(Let a child pour in some*

water.) Jose prayed to God. He asked a lot of questions to learn more about God. Jose jumped up every Sunday and begged to go to church. Jose loved Jesus, and Jesus loved Jose. *(Draw a smiling face on the cup.)* Jose grew and grew and grew as a Christian. *(Have a child put in a flower.)* Soon Jose's life looked like this beautiful plant. *(Set down the potted plant.)* He shared the love of Jesus with everyone around him.

Questions

- How did you feel when the little plants in the cups were ruined?
- Tell about a time when something kept you from spending time with Jesus.
- How can you be more like the last plant that grew and grew?

Story Extension Ideas

- Have the children each plant a flower seed in a cup to keep. Have them cut out a heart and copy the following poem onto it. Glue the heart to the cup.

  Make my heart soft and ready so I can grow true and steady,
  So I can share your love with all while I'm growing strong and tall.

- Give children each a seed to hold in their hands while the children pray for God to help them grow spiritually. Have the children each fashion their own seed package out of construction paper. They can write on paper "seeds" the words from Isaiah 55:11.

Other Story Possibilities

- Let your children re-create the story of the wise and foolish builders in Matthew 7:24-29. Use wooden toy blocks nestled in sand for one house. Make the house on the rock out of plastic blocks that fasten together (like Duplos). Build the homes in plastic containers, and pour water on them. You can even write the verse from Matthew 7:24 on the plastic blocks in wipe-off crayons (found in teachers' supply stores).
- Let the children bring in empty cereal boxes and cover them with butcher paper. They can build while you tell the story of the tower of Babel (Genesis 11:1-9). The children can then write the story on the blocks or draw pictures of it.

K-3

Traditional Storytelling

What is the most timeless, tested, and powerful technique for telling stories? Yes, traditional storytelling! Jesus, our Creator, knew this and touched the hearts of his hearers of old (and today) with parables and true tales. This powerful, ancient art is still available to us today. Seeing eager eyes swallowing every detail and then hearing the children recounting them to you years later is a potent vitalizer for any teacher. This account of the good shepherd is analyzed to teach you some techniques behind translating God's Word for children.

The Story

The Good Shepherd, Matthew 18:10-14; Luke 13:1-7; and John 10:1-18 and 27-30

The Point

Jesus is our good shepherd.

The Materials

Index card for outline

Preparation

The key to telling any story well is to know the story well—inside out, upside down, and backwards. But it is not rote memory! Read the accounts in the Bible passages listed above. Then carefully read the story below three times. Write out an outline on an index card. Try to tell the tale to a mirror. Use the outline if you get stuck. Practice again, and pray for God to speak through you. Gather the kids on a carpet, use plenty of eye contact, and enjoy the experience.

Let's Begin

Loving LouLou

The introduction must capture the children's attention right away. Set the stage with conflict, dialogue, suspense, or even a question. You might say, "I'd like to tell you this story, but I'm afraid you aren't old enough." Or "I'd like to tell you this story, but it may make you cry." The kids will beg you to continue.

Baaaaa. Baaa. Bbbaaa. CJ, the shepherd, looked up. That rotten LouLou was at it again, kicking the little lambs so that she could eat the sweetest grass herself. Oh, that LouLou! Not only was she fat from stealing, she was mean, too. To show the other sheep that she was boss, she'd strut up to a weaker sheep, stare right at it, lower her head, and then bam, bam, bam—she'd butt her head into the poor sheep until it ran away.

> The number one rule in storytelling is "Show, don't tell." Don't just tell the children "LouLou was rotten." Tell what she did that was rotten. Don't just say, "She was the boss." Tell how she proved it.

"At least I've named you right," CJ scolded LouLou while he petted the frightened lambs. "You sure live up to what your name means—"famous woman warrior." LouLou only chewed on some tasty yellow flowers and snorted at her shepherd. Even though LouLou was getting older, she wasn't about to give up being the leader of the flock.

> Use dialogue to get into the character's thoughts and feelings. Underline the dialogue in yellow. Use a deeper voice for a man and perhaps an accent for another character. Change pitch and speed to provide variety and clarity for your listeners.

The next day, CJ was rounding up the sheep to move them to a fresh field. CJ patted each sheep as it skipped out the gate to the rich, green pasture. He called his sheep by name: "Lolita, Snow Ball, Cream Puff, Big Mama, Sissy, Sassy, Black Boots…now where was LouLou?" CJ wondered.

> Check out the action in this paragraph that has comparatively little drama. Lively verbs keep a story alive—glanced, squeezed, bucked, and snorted. Go through this entire story, and underline all the verbs in green. How many are passive? Very few. Use a thesaurus to change weak verbs to more exciting words. However, be sure to use words that children will understand. Remember, the Word of God is living and active. Let's share that energy with the kids.

"LouLou!" CJ glanced up just in time to see LouLou squeeze through the broken fence. Just beyond the fence were steep cliffs. "LouLou, get back here," CJ huffed as he ran to her and pulled her back in with his staff. She bucked and snorted and even tried to butt CJ's staff with her hard head. CJ mended the fence and laid a board across the broken gate. "LouLou, LouLou." CJ shook his head. "You give me more trouble than all the other ninety-nine sheep in my flock. Don't you realize that my job is to take care of you? Why do you try to escape to the cliffs? There is danger out there." He rubbed her soft wool. "If you would only learn to follow me, you'd be much happier. Now go on with the other sheep, you goofy ewe. I still love you."

> Use alliteration to tickle the children's ears—spit, sparked, and sputtered. Can you find more? Create a scene with descriptive adjectives—starry, happy, warm. But use them only to paint a picture for the children. Don't overuse adjectives. This paragraph depicts a peaceful scene, but nowhere does it say, "All was peaceful." Show, don't tell.

That night, CJ waited until the last ember from the fire spit, sparked, and sputtered out. He looked up to the starry sky. He heard the bells his sheep wore gently jingle and a baby lamb bleating for more of mama's milk. CJ took one more glance at his happy flock. Asking God to protect his sheep throughout the night, CJ pulled up his blanket and fell asleep. Baby lambs nestled next to mama's wonderful, warm wool. The flock rested. All but one.

> Pausing for emphasis can be quite effective. Just as music needs rests, so do words. Don't be afraid of silence. Use it to accentuate an important point.

Guess who? *(Pause.)* Yes, Lady LouLou tiptoed to the fence and nudged every wobbly spot. She butted and wiggled and poked and prodded until—aha!—a board gave way. LouLou picked up her black hoofs and wriggled through the broken fence, out into the dark night. *(Drop voice.)* Alone. *(Pause.)*

> Why did LouLou escape? Give every character in your story a motive. This shows respect for the intelligence of the children in your audience and moves the story along. Was LouLou simply being ornery? If you show the "whys" behind the "whats," your listeners will empathize with the protagonist and possibly the antagonist, causing them to increase their mental involvement.

Freedom! LouLou didn't know which way to turn first. Should she find the brook to splash about in? Perhaps she should play with the fireflies? What was over that ridge? She'd always wanted to know. She would know. LouLou tramped through briars and bushes. Her clean white coat got snagged with thorns. She climbed up the mountain to the top of the ridge, huffing and puffing. She peered through the darkness, trying to see the valley below. LouLou thought to herself, "When I get to the bottom of this mountain, it will be daylight. Then I'll see what's here."

> Children love sounds. Onomatopoeia—words that sound like their sounds—is a fun way to bring life to your story. Words like "ring," "clank," "thump," or "splat" tickle children's ears. How many such words can you find in this story? Include the children whenever possible. Have them join you for a loud, "Baaaa, baaaaa" when LouLou calls for CJ. Animate your actions. Stick your feet up in the air. Climb the mountain; huff and puff. When the shepherd names and then counts his flock, touch each child on the head.

LouLou began to inch her way down the steep mountain, her tiny hoofs crunching and wobbling on the loose rocks. All of a sudden, a rock shot out from under her. Crash! LouLou slipped. She tumbled doowwnn. She rolled over and over, bouncing off tree stumps (thump!) and slamming into rocks (whump!). Baaaa. BAAAAAAA. Baaa. Oof. LouLou finally came to a halt, on the bottom of the valley. LouLou lay on her back, her feet sticking up in the cold night air. She stared up into the black sky. Her white wool was ripped and tattered with brown splotches of mud and red patches from bleeding cuts.

The harder LouLou tried to roll over and get up, the more her body got stuck into the rut. She kicked her feet; she wiggled; she strained her neck. No luck. LouLou was stuck in the muck. I'll just holler for help, she thought. She gathered her breath and let out her loudest baaaaaa! "There," LouLou said to herself, "CJ will be here in no time."

Repetition is to a story what salt is to food. Repeating phrases or words is like an echo reverberating in the child's mind. Sprinkle repetitions in patterns of threes throughout your story for a savory effect.

LouLou waited. And waited. And waited. Finally she heard something. It was a snap of a twig. LouLou bleated again loudly so CJ would know where she was in the darkness. Baaaaaa! She strained her ears, waiting to hear the sound of CJ scolding her.

A little research can add realistic details to your story. (For example, sheep become stuck in a position called casting). Scripture gives us the bottom line, allowing us to fill in the rest of the lines with exciting details. Always try to appeal to the five senses: taste, touch, hearing, sight, and smell. Go through the story, and underline in red all the sensory appeal that gives this story life.

Snap. Grrrrr. LouLou froze. It wasn't CJ who had come to get her. She peered through the darkness and saw two yellow eyes peer back. She kicked with all her might, frantically pawing the air. But her woolly coat was now drenched with dew, making it heavy and even more impossible for her to get up. Morning light started to brighten the sky. LouLou could see that the yellow eyes belonged to a wolf!

The wolf stepped closer. He could smell the sticky, sweet blood. His tongue licked his lips. GRRrrrrr.

Pacing is important to convey emotion. Tell this part of the story slowly, picking up the pace as you go. Count deliberately, building tension. You'll have the children on the edge of their seats, silently imploring you to hurry up and save LouLou. Let the audience sweat it out. Involving them emotionally is what it's all about.

Back at the pasture, CJ sat stirring his coffee. He looked up and saw three black-winged birds circling in slow motion out over the valley—vultures. CJ realized that in the night something must have die...died. He leaped to his feet, splashing his coffee to the ground. CJ raced around his flock counting every sheep he owned. One, two, three, four, five...thirty-six, thirty-seven...eighty-two...Wait. That lamb was hiding behind his mother. Start again. One, two, three, four, five...sixty-eight, ninety-six, ninety-seven, ninety-eight, ninety-nine. One was missing.

CJ raced along the fence. Oh, no. There was the board she had pushed down. He picked up a piece of wool that had been snagged on the fence. LouLou! He knew it. CJ ran back to the fire for his staff. He left the ninety-nine sheep alone in the pasture and jumped over the fence, yelling, "LOULOU! Where are you?"

> **Use motion to elicit emotion. Climbing motions, whacking at invisible briars, and shielding your eyes, as the shepherd does, bring the story from the past to the present—where children live.**

CJ climbed over hills and mountains. He struggled through briar patches. His throat was raw from yelling. CJ followed the vultures to the top of the ridge. He shielded his eyes in the bright morning sun and stared down the mountain to the valley. He gasped. There was LouLou, her feet in the air, lying still. And who was next to LouLou? Yes, the wolf.

> **You may want to tone down the following violent scene for K-1 listeners and simply say that CJ fought the wolf. The two struggled until the wolf realized that the shepherd would never quit.**

He jumped into action, skidding down the mountain. CJ tried to grab a rock and hold onto his staff. He landed in the valley with a thud. CJ raced over to LouLou but stopped in his tracks. Grrrrr. The wolf had a mouth full of wool in his mouth and was crouching down, staring at CJ. CJ threw the rock at the wolf. The wolf pounced on CJ, knocking him to the ground. CJ grabbed for his staff, but the wolf caught his arm with dagger-like teeth. Pain surged through CJ, but he fought the wolf. The wolf bit him over and over, but CJ beat him with his staff. Finally, the wolf realized that this shepherd would never quit. He slunk back into the woods, leaving a trail of blood.

CJ panted and turned back to LouLou. His heart hurt worse than the gashes on his arms and face. "LouLou, my love," CJ said, rolling her over. *(Pause for a moment.)* He heard a sigh and then a weak bbbaaaaa.

> **A well-told tale need not include the moral of the story at the end. This is what you want the children to discover for themselves. See if they understand by asking pointed questions after the story. Their answers will solidify in their minds what the Holy Spirit is teaching them.**

"LouLou, you're alive!" The good shepherd hugged her, his eyes wet with tears. He rubbed her legs until she could stand up. She bleated and rubbed her head on CJ's belly. He laughed. "Come on, Lady LouLou. We're going home." CJ bent down and wiggled under LouLou until that big sheep was on his shoulders. He trudged up the mountain with LouLou having the ride of her life. "When we get back to the pasture, I'm having a Welcome Home LouLou Party for you!" he said. And he did.

Questions

- The shepherd had ninety-nine other sheep. Why did CJ leave those sheep to go searching for LouLou?
- How did the shepherd feel when he found LouLou?
- How are we like sheep?
- How is Jesus like a good shepherd?

Story Extension Ideas

- Play a game of Lost and Found to experience the Father's joy in finding his lost children. Have each child make a paper sheep and cover it with cotton. Have children each write their names on their sheep. Hide the sheep outdoors, and then assign each child a partner's sheep to look for. Or let one child hide and share the happiness she or he felt in being found.
- Invite someone to come to your class to share his or her testimony. Bake a cake and have a Lost and Found Party. Let the children share the celebration by sharing their own before- and after-Christ stories.

Other Story Possibilities

- Any Bible story can be studied and shared with an audience. Think of the details you could add to the story of Eutychus' fall into slumber and out the window (Acts 20:7-12). No one in your audience will dare to nod off after this tale is told!
- Jesus' casting demons into pigs (Mark 5:1-20) is a ready-made story filled with drama, emotion, and mystery. Try telling it from the viewpoint of the possessed man, getting into the whys of his condition and his feelings before, during, and after his encounter with the living Son of God.

K-1

Food Faces

Big sugar cookies become the pages, and icing squeezed into faces becomes the words. Simple faces expressing different emotions will tell this tasty tale. The children can take home a cookie to share the love of Jesus and retell the story to someone else. When a Bible story is in three out of four Gospels, let's dig in!

The Story

Jesus Welcomes the Children, Matthew 19:13-15; Mark 10:13-16; and Luke 18:15-17

The Point

Children are important to Jesus.

The Materials

Ingredients for sugar cookie dough or several packages of refrigerated sugar cookie dough (three large cookies for each child), icing tinted to any darker color with food coloring, snack-sized plastic bags, and scissors

Preparation

If you make your own cookie dough, the dough needs to be refrigerated for one to two hours before it can be cut and baked, so you may want to plan accordingly. To extend this activity, the children can help add the ingredients and mix the dough at the first session. At the next session, the kids can roll out the dough and bake it. If time allows for the cookies to bake and cool, you can tell the story that same day. Tint the icing, and put it into snack-sized resealable bags. Snip a corner from the bag to create a simple pastry bag. Each child will need a bag of icing.

Directions

Bake cookies according to the recipe or to the package directions. Allow the cookies to cool completely before telling the story. Have the children work in pairs, taking turns to create the six faces described in the story on the cookies using the icing.

Let's Begin

This story comes out of three books in the Bible—Matthew, Mark, and Luke. It is super important because God wants us to know that children are super important. Today I'm going to tell you the story in a sweet way. Gather around the table and listen. With your partner, take turns making cookie faces. I'll show you what to put on each face.

Cookie 1: *(Squeeze out a happy face.)*

Sarah came running to her mother saying, "Mama, he's here! He's here! He finally came to our town!"

Mother said, "Who is here, Sarah?"

Sarah said, jumping up and down, "Jesus! Jesus is here!"

Her younger brother, Joash, came running in, "Mama, pweaze, me go see Jesus!"

Mother said, "Jesus is a busy man doing important things. He may not have time for a bunch of little children."

"Please, Mama. We hear that Jesus loves little children," Joash and Sarah begged her.

Mother smiled. "OK," she said.

When Mama, Sarah, and Joash got to the marketplace, there was a bustling crowd around Jesus. People were bringing babies and children to Jesus.

Cookie 2: *(Squeeze out a smiley face and a beard.)*

Jesus welcomed all the children—the crippled ones, the sick ones, the mean ones, the nice ones, the dark-skinned and the light-skinned children, too. The air was filled with the happy sounds of giggles and laughter. Babies would stop crying just as soon as Jesus picked them up. Mothers said, "Jesus, please bless my Nathaniel. And my Leah."

Jesus put his hands on the children's head. To Abby, he said, "God bless you, Abby. God, our Father, loves you. I do too." Then Abby skipped away, telling everyone how lucky she was.

Jesus prayed for some of the children. When Joel climbed onto Jesus' lap, Jesus held him close, shut his eyes, and prayed, "Dear Father, please help Joel to grow up into a mighty man of God." Joel looked at Jesus with big, brown eyes, hugged his neck, and whispered, "Thank you, Jesus."

(Go around the table, hugging all the children, reminding them of your love and how much Jesus loves them.)

Jesus opened his arms to all the children. Sarah squeezed her way through the crowd and jumped into Jesus' arms. He gave her a huge hug. Sarah wished the hug would last forever. Then she heard Joash. He was tugging at Jesus' robe. "Me too, me too. Me want Jesus too!"

Jesus picked Joash up and put him on his lap.

Cookie 3: *(Squeeze a mad face onto this cookie.)*

Just then, an angry voice rose over the giggles, "Go away! Move along! Leave Jesus alone!" One of Jesus' disciples was pushing his way into the crowd of children and mothers.

Another disciple joined him, yelling, "Don't you think Jesus has more important things to do than bother with a bunch of little kids?"

"Go home! Jesus is tired," scolded another disciple.

Cookie 4: *(Squeeze out a sad face.)*

Sarah's happy face was crushed. The best day in her life was turning into the worst. Mothers pulled their babies closer to themselves. Some of the children started to cry. Joash slipped off Jesus' lap, snuffing up sobs.

Mother reached for Joash and Sarah's hand, "Come on children, I was afraid of th…"

Cookie 5: *(Squeeze out a talking face with a beard.)*

Jesus stood up. "Stop," he said in a loud voice. Everyone froze, even the disciples. He scolded the disciples, "Do not stop the children from coming to me. Ever. Don't you understand? The kingdom of heaven is made up of people whose hearts are like children." The disciples dropped their heads and quietly slipped away.

Cookie 6: *(Squeeze out a big happy face.)* Jesus held open his arms again. He said in a voice for all to hear—a voice so clear and true that we can hear him today, "Let the little children come to me."

Yahoo! All the children came running back to Jesus. He wiped away their tears. The party went on for hours. Joash and Sarah chattered all the way home about their day. They couldn't wait to tell Papa about their day with Jesus. After all, it had been their happiest day.

Questions

- How do you think Jesus feels about children?
- How do you think Jesus feel about you?
- How do you feel when you know someone loves you?
- How can you let other children know how Jesus feels about them?

Story Extension Ideas

- Decorate a bulletin board to look like the arms of Jesus. Put a picture of each child on it. In large letters write the words, "How does a child come to Jesus?" Draw a bubble, and record the children's poignant answers in their own words in the bubble corresponding to their names.
- Photocopy the pictures of the kids, and have them each cut and glue their picture onto a small magnet. Glue a picture of Jesus to a large magnet. Lay this all on a cookie sheet, and let the children experiment with coming to Jesus. Talk about the magnetic attraction of a savior who loves us.

Other Story Possibilities

- Other stories can be told using simple facial expressions on cookies. Tell the story of Jesus feeding the five thousand (Mark 6:30-44). Include smiles for the people learning from Jesus, sad faces for their hunger, a talking face for Jesus' command about the fish and loaves, and surprised faces from the disciples. (Happy faces for the leftovers!)
- Tell the story of David and Jonathan's friendship as recorded in 1 Samuel 20. Use smiling faces for the kinship, angry faces from Saul, talking faces when they plan, surprised faces from Jonathan, and sad faces when the friends must part.

2-5

Unfinished Story

What would life be like if biblical characters had changed their responses to God? Let your children rewrite history. This technique is wonderfully flexible and can be used with so many other Bible stories. It woos the children into the stories by engaging their imaginations and helping them face Biblical reality. What will their life's response be to Jesus' challenge, "Come follow me"? Will they become sad and walk away? Will they follow? Now is the time to plant the seeds of commitment.

The Story

The Rich Young Ruler, Luke 18:18-30; Matthew 19:16-22; and Mark 10:17-22

The Point

We need to choose to follow Jesus.

The Materials

For second- and third-graders, one copy of the story for each child, paper, and pencil. For fourth-and-fifth graders, Bibles of the same translation, paper, pencil, and self-adhesive notes

Preparation

Read the biblical accounts in Matthew, Mark, and Luke to familiarize yourself with the story. For children in grades two and three, photocopy the handout titled "The Rich Young Ruler" (p. 128) so that each person has a copy. For children in grades four and five, use self-adhesive notes to cover the verses following Jesus' words to the young man: "Come and follow me."

Directions

Tell the children they will be making up two endings to the story. Read the handout for the second- and third-graders, and ask for volunteers from the fourth- and fifth-graders to take turns reading sentences from the Bible passage. Have the children write down their endings and read their composite story aloud.

THE RICH YOUNG RULER

Jesus started to walk away from the crowd.
A young man ran up to Jesus.
He fell in the dusty road on his knees.
This man didn't care that his fancy robe was getting dirty.
He didn't care what people thought.
He cared about the question that was burning in his heart.
He said, "Good teacher. What must I do to live forever in heaven?"
Jesus said, "Why do you call me good? No one is good—except God.
You know the Ten Commandments:
Do not kill, do not steal, do not lie.
Respect your father and mother."
He said, "I have kept all these since I was a boy.
Still, there is something missing in my life.
All my money and power have not filled
the hunger in my soul.
What is missing?"
Jesus looked at him and loved him.
Jesus saw that he wanted to know God's heart.
"One thing stands between you and God," Jesus said.
The young man's mind raced.
What could it be?
Would he have to work harder?
Earn more money?
Jesus looked into his eyes.
Jesus said, "Go, sell everything you have.
Give your money to the poor.
You will become rich with God.
Then come, follow me."

Let's Begin

What did the young man do? Let fourth- and fifth-graders work in teams to write a response. For first- and second-graders, write their responses on a board or large paper. As the story proceeds, use some of the following questions to guide their imaginations. Give the man and your story a name. Describe the man's life, his work and his wealth. How did he feel about selling his things? What would his life be like without his things? Then let the teams read their versions. Finally read the New Testament version of the story, and compare it to their responses.

Questions

- How do you think the young man felt when Jesus asked him to sell all he had?
- How would you respond to Jesus if this were his request of you?

Story Extension Ideas

- Have the kids look up 1 Corinthians 13:3, Matthew 22:35-39 and Ephesians 2:8-9. Ask them to write a letter to the young man asking him to reconsider his decision. The letter could be from Peter, describing what an exciting adventure it is to follow Jesus.
- Give the children an opportunity to give some of what they have to the poor. Hold a garage sale for the church sponsored by your class. Select a charity to which you can donate the proceeds. It would be wonderful if the children could accompany you as you give the check to a local homeless shelter, needy family, or children's home.

Other Story Possibilities

- Read the story of Sennacherib's threat in 2 Kings 18. What would have happened if King Hezekiah had surrendered to the king of Assyria? Read the real response in the following chapter.
- Suppose Abigail hadn't intervened when Nabal spurned David's request for food for his men. Read 1 Samuel 25:1-17 and let the students rewrite history.

K-5

Slide Show

A slide show will allow beautiful stories to be shared with audiences of all ages and sizes. They are captivated because their attention is so focused and their auditory and visual needs are simultaneously saturated. And the parable of the lost son returning to his loving father is too rich a treasure to be buried in a book! Fourth- and fifth-graders can produce the show to share with others.

The Story

The Prodigal Son, Luke 15:11-31

The Point

God always welcomes us.

The Materials

Twenty plastic slide mounts (found in camera stores); one sheet of transparency film; fine-line markers; colored permanent markers; slide projector and tray; and a smooth, white wall or screen. Optional: background music, a small flashlight

Preparation

Using the blank frames provided on page 133, draw twenty simple line drawings as indicated in the story. Reduce them, and photocopy the page of drawings onto transparency film. Cut around the dotted lines of the pictures. Gently slide the transparencies into the slide mounts. Have the fourth- and fifth-graders highlight portions of the line drawings with permanent markers to add a touch of color. Number the slides, and load them into the tray. Make sure the room can be darkened. Fourth- and fifth-graders could read the script aloud. Practice several times before presenting it to a large group. You may even want to add music.

Directions

Keep a small flashlight handy to read your script by. Watch the slides to see if they correspond to the text.

Let's Begin

SLIDE 1: Three men with a barn in the background

Jesus was the king of storytelling, and this story he told is an all-time favorite. There was a man who had a farm and two sons. The sons had almost grown into men themselves. Let's call the two brothers Jesse and Jonathan. Now Jonathan was a good, hard worker. When the roosters crowed each morning, Jonathan jumped out of bed. He went right to work, roaming the fields to see if any cows had given birth through the night.

"Jonathan," his father said, "You make me proud to have such a fine helper."

SLIDE 2: Two men, one with a smile, one with a frown

Jonathan smiled, but Jesse only rolled his eyes and dragged a comb through his hair. "I hate this old farm," he said. "I'd like to go to the city and really live!"

Jonathan asked, "Where on earth would you get the money to do that?"

SLIDE 3: Brother talking to father

Jesse looked at his father. Jesse knew that his father had a big wallet and a big heart. "Dad," Jesse said, "I know you are saving money for us for when you die, but you may not die for a long time. Is there any way you could give me my money now?"

The father stroked his beard, "Hhmm, there is some truth to what you say. All right, Jesse, you may have your money now."

SLIDE 4: Brother with bundle and sack at belt

"Thanks, Dad." Jesse hugged him. He ran to his room and threw all his clothes into a bundle. Jesse hugged his dad again and stuffed the money into a special sack around his belt. "Goodbye!" he waved.

SLIDE 5: Sad-faced father

Jesse's father watched his son mount his horse and gallop off down the path. A tear rolled down his cheek. "I remember his first step," the father thought. "Jesse has always been on the move. I just didn't expect him to grow up and be gone so fast." With a long, slow sigh, he trudged back to work in the fields.

SLIDE 6: Brother with big smile

As Jesse trotted down the rode, he yelled to the cows, "Yahoo! I'm free!" Their big, brown eyes just stared back.

SLIDE 7: A city

Jesse loved the crowded, busy city. He made a lot of friends.

SLIDE 8: A bottle and a glass

He drank a lot of wine.

SLIDE 9: Lots of people

He went to a lot of wild parties.

SLIDE 10: Rings and necklaces

He bought a lot of pretty things for a lot of pretty girls.

SLIDE 11: Brother with pigs

But one day, he reached into his money bag and said, "Oh, rats, I'm out of money. I guess I'll have to (gulp) work. Bummer." Jesse tried to find a job, but no one needed him. His stomach growled. Finally he found a job feeding pigs.

SLIDE 12: Brother thinking of father and farm

"Back on a farm," he grumbled. He threw the pigs some smelly scraps and watched them gobble it up. Jesse's stomach growled again. But no one gave him anything to eat. The next day when he tossed old gnawed-on corncobs to the pigs, he thought, I wish I could fill my belly with a piece of their corn. Then he jumped up. "Wait a minute! Why am I jealous of these pigs when I could go home? Even the men who work for my father eat better than I do. I'm out of here."

SLIDE 13: Brother walking with head down

As Jesse walked down many roads, he practiced what he would say when he saw his father: "I'm sorry, Dad. I'm not good enough to be called your son. Make me like one of your hired men...I'm sorry, Dad, I'm not good enough to be called your son..."

SLIDE 14: Happy father with brother in background

But while he was still a long way off, his father saw him. His heart was filled with love and pity.

SLIDE 15: Brother and father hugging

The father ran to his son, threw his arms around him and kissed him.

SLIDE 16: Brother with sandals and robe

Jesse said, "I'm sorry, Dad. I'm not good enough to be called your son..."

But his father said to his servants, "Quick! Bring out a fancy robe for my son. Put a ring on his finger and a new pair of sandals on his feet. Bring that fat roast I've been saving; we are going to celebrate! We'll have a huge, happy, wonderful party!"

SLIDE 17: Two confused servants

His servants' jaws dropped. They remembered the long days when the father worried about his son. They saw that the son had spent all his father's money and was now standing there in rags. They looked at each other and shrugged their shoulders.

SLIDE 18: A feast

"Don't you see?" the father said, hugging Jesse to him. "It's like Jesse was dead but now he's alive! He was lost and is found." So they had a party. They ate. They laughed. They danced to the music.

SLIDE 19: Angry brother

Jonathan came home from working in the fields. "What's going on here?" he asked. When he found out that Jesse was home and the party was for him, he burned with anger.

His father came out and said, "Come in and join the celebration."

Jonathan folded his arms and frowned. "Look! All these years I've worked hard for you, and you never gave ME a party!"

SLIDE 20: Father and son

"My son," the father said, "don't you see? You are always with me and I love you. But we HAD to celebrate and be glad. Your brother was dead and is alive; he was lost and is found."

Questions

- How do you feel when you lose something very important to you?
- How is that like the young man who left his father?
- How does God feel when someone turns from him?
- When someone turns away from God, how can they come back to him?

Story Extension Ideas

- Have a Lost and Found party. Let the kids create invitations using verses such as Isaiah 1:18, Jeremiah 3:12, Hosea 12:1 and Matthew 11:28. Hide chocolate coins around the rooms, and after all the coins have been found, celebrate with a roast and the works.
- Make a life-sized board game having a road of stones (made from sheets of construction paper) that leads from the farm to the city. Have older kids leave home and advance down the road, from stone to stone, by listing characteristics of Jesse, such as "I want to see what life is like on the other side," for each step along the road. They return home by listing Jesse's thoughts, such as "Life in the fast lane is sometimes too fast."

Other Story Possibilities

Once you learn how to draw simple line drawings (similar to those found in Good News Bible: Today's English Version), you can tell any Bible story on slides. Fill in the drawings on the empty pages, reduce by 30 percent, copy onto transparencies, and slip them into slide mounts. Or let the children draw their own pictures.

- You may use some of the same slides to tell the story of the twin brothers Esau and Jacob (Genesis 25–28) or of Cain and Abel, another set of infamous brothers.
- In Mark 10:35-45, we see two brothers, James and John, vying for power positions.

K-3

Walk-Through Drama

In this exciting storytelling technique, the audience moves with the actors from room to room as the story unfolds just a few feet in front of them. This way, sets can remain intact, and people will have time to think as they move from one scene to the next. This drama is interactive and filled with many scents, tastes, and sights to reflect the joy of the risen Jesus.

The Story

The Easter Story, Matthew 26–28

The Point

Jesus lives!

The Materials

Bible-time tunics for Mary and Jesus, large bowl, perfume in a clay jar, flashlight, juice and cups, handcuffs (made out of black paper or rope), hammer, masking tape, vinegar, crown of thorns, sponge, paper pieces or self-adhesive notes, ten strips of cloth, red pen for each child, sheet for tomb, real or artificial flowers, floral air freshener spray, jar with shortening, spices (such as nutmeg, allspice, and cinnamon), and spoons. Optional: Crown of thorns. (This can be made out of real thorns, twisted and tied together with thin wire.)

Preparation

Choose a Jesus and a Mary to travel with the groups of children. Mary should be an adult, but you may choose an older child as Jesus. Plan on bringing in groups of no more than ten children at a time. The "tour" takes about twenty minutes. You will need helpers stationed in Rooms 2 and 3. Practice your script and prepare the rooms. The rooms should be near one another. They needn't be emptied of their contents, but distracting objects should be set aside. In Room 1, you'll only need one chair and the jar of perfume. In Room 2, you'll need a table and a flashlight. The room needs to become dark. Have the juice and cups near the door. In Room 3, you'll need a cross made of tape on one wall. There should be room for Jesus to stand beside the cross. The crown of thorns, handcuffs, vinegar, sponge, hammer, and self-adhesive notes are used here. Room 4 needs to have a cave/tomb large enough for Jesus made from several chairs covered with a sheet. Have the strips of cloth near the cave. You'll need something to serve as a rock, perhaps a chair or a marker board. Flowers and the air freshener are hidden out of sight. Room 5 works best if there is a window with a shade or curtain to peer out of. You will need the jar with shortening, spices, and spoons here. If you practice, prepare, and pray, God will bless your presentation.

Let's Begin

INTRODUCTION: A Walk Through the Garden

Mary: *(Standing outside Room 1)* Welcome to "A Walk Through the Garden." My name is Mary of Magdalene. What happened in my life was so amazing that people are still talking about it two thousand years later. I was at one time a *(Hangs head.)* sinful woman. I won't even tell you about all of the terrible things I have done.

Then one day, I heard that Jesus was coming to my town. Jesus! I had heard how he had made sick people well and taught the way to know God. He even raised one man back from the dead! I grabbed the only thing that I had that was special to me, this jar of perfume, and I dashed out the door. I ran to the house where Jesus was staying. Come on, let's go see Jesus! *(Runs to the first door and enters.)*

ROOM 1: The Annointing at the Home of Simon

(Jesus is seated on a chair.)

Mary: I burst through the door, and there was Jesus. I saw that no one had even bothered to wash his feet. In Israel, we have so much dust on our streets that people usually wash their feet when they come into a house. *(Kneels at Jesus' feet.)* Jesus, Jesus, I cried, I am so sorry for my sins.

I wept at Jesus' feet and dried the tears with my hair. Then I poured my very expensive perfume on his feet. *(Pretends to pour perfume on Jesus' feet.)* It was the only thing I could offer him. Then he said something I didn't really understand.

Jesus: You have done a beautiful thing to me. You are preparing for the day I will be buried. Your sins are forgiven. Come and follow me.

Mary: I did follow Jesus, everywhere. You can too. Come and smell the sweet scent of forgiveness. *(Passes around the jar of perfume.)*

ROOM 2: The Garden of Gethsemane

Mary: The night before Jesus died, he went with his disciples to a garden to pray.

(Helper shines a flashlight in the darkened room on Jesus.)

Jesus: *(Kneeling)* Dear Father, my soul is filled with sadness. I don't want to drink that cup of death. But I will do your will. I will die for the forgiveness of all people.

Mary: You will probably never be asked to die for your faith, but God does have a cup of obedience for you to drink. God may ask you not to tease someone or to obey when you don't want to. We'll pretend that this cup of juice is what God asks you to do. *(Pours a cup of grape juice for everyone.)*

ROOM 3: Arrest and Crucifixion

Mary: They arrested Jesus *(Helper puts handcuffs on Jesus.)* and beat him. He had done nothing wrong—not one sin. But the leaders were jealous because so many people followed Jesus. They whipped him and put a crown of thorns on his head. *(Helper puts crown of thorns on Jesus.)* Then they put Jesus on the cross. Cruel soldiers filled a sponge with vinegar and shoved it at Jesus. *(Pours vinegar* *on a sponge and lets the children smell it.)* Jesus could have called his Father and had hundreds of angels come and rescue him. But he didn't. Jesus loves you this much. *(Jesus stretches out his arms to the wall. Helper turns the lights down low, then slowly pounds hammer on a table as* ***Mary*** *speaks.)*

We all have sinned. We all have left God to follow our own way. Jesus died to take away your sins. Write your name on this paper and stick it to the cross.

(Each child writes his or her name on a self-adhesive note and sticks it to the cross next to Jesus. Older students can write down a sin they struggle with.)

When Jesus died, *(Jesus hangs his head and closes his eyes.)* an earthquake shook the land. *(Helper rattles chairs.)* The soldiers who crucified Jesus shouted, "Surely, this was the Son of God."

(Jesus should move to the burial room and lie down before children come in.)

ROOM 4: Burial

Mary: The soldiers took Jesus down from the cross, and a follower called Joseph wrapped Jesus' body tightly and laid him in a tomb. Please help me wrap Jesus up in these cloth strips. *(Wraps Jesus.)* It was awful to watch the soldiers take my beloved Jesus and roll the rock across the tomb. I need one person to push this stone in front of the tomb. Now, everyone, take a red pen, and make one dot on each of your palms. This is to remind you that Jesus Christ loves you and died for you.

(Older children can write "Jesus died" on their left hands and "for me" on their right hands. While everyone proceeds to Room 5, Jesus quietly stands, moves the rock away, and puts flowers all around the tomb. He sprays the room with floral freshener. Then he hides behind the tomb.)

ROOM 5: The Disciples' Hidden Room

Mary: The followers of Jesus, called disciples, were all together in a room, praying, crying, and keeping watch to make sure the soldiers wouldn't find them. Will you help me show what it was like? I need one disciple to look out this window. The rest of us will kneel down. *(Spends a brief time praying for the protection of the disciples and expressing sorrow and confusion over Jesus' death.)* Tomorrow is Sunday, and I have to put spices and perfume on Jesus' body. Please help me mix these spices. We'll use this on Jesus' dead body, as we do with all our dead. *(Have all the children add spices to the bowl of shortening and take turns mixing it.)* We still have the problem of rolling away that huge rock. It will take many strong men. Let's go. It's Sunday morning.

ROOM 4: The Empty Tomb

Mary: Why, look, all the flowers have bloomed! Oh, the rock is rolled away! *(Looks in.)* He isn't here! Look for yourself! *(Everyone peers into the empty tomb.)* The grave clothes are still here. *(Pulls out the strips of cloth.)* What could have happened?

Jesus: *(Bursts out from behind tomb.)* I HAVE RISEN! Nothing could keep me in the grave, not even death. And nothing can stop my love for you. I died and rose again for you. Now, will you live for me?

Mary: The day I was forgiven, I started living for Jesus who died and now lives for me. I hope you, too, will give your life to Christ. Please take a flower to remember your walk through the garden. Goodbye.

Questions

- How did the disciples feel when they thought Jesus was dead?
- How did that change when they discovered he had risen?
- Easter celebrates that Jesus lives. What can you do at Easter to show how glad you are Jesus lives?

Story Extensions

- Take a helium balloon, and draw the face and body of Jesus on it. Make the face with a beard and closed eyes. Put it in a box, and have the children use white crepe paper to wrap it up, as though it were Jesus in his tomb. Go outside. Let the children help you rip open the "tomb" of Jesus to see him rise. He's alive!
- Let each child cut a cross out of paper and write "Jesus is alive!" on it. The child then folds up the cross and places it in a plastic Easter egg. The children can carefully dip their plastic eggs into melted candy coating. Before the coating hardens, let them decorate the eggs with candy sprinkles. When the coating has hardened, the kids can wrap the eggs in pretty Mylar paper and ribbon and distribute them to special people on Easter day.

Other Story Possibilities

- The story of Esther can be adapted to a play and acted out in these five rooms: a palace, Esther's home, the king's harem, the open provincial town square, and the gallows.
- A Christmas Walk-Through Drama would be wonderful for a Christmas party. The kids could go from one room with the angel Gabriel to the next room of Joseph's home to Bethlehem where they are turned away at the inn. The fourth room could be the stable where Jesus is born, and the fifth could be the fields of the shepherds, complete with glow-in-the-dark stars.

K-3

Verse Rehearsed

Use a Bible verse to teach the Bible? Hmm? It may not sound novel, but it is and it works! Scripture becomes living and active, judging the attitudes of two very human figures—Ananias and Sapphira. The verse exhorting us to "keep our tongue from evil and lips from speaking lies" is woven throughout this amazing Bible story. Without knowing it, the children learn a Bible verse.

The Story

Ananias and Sapphira, Acts 5:1-11

The Point

Speaking the truth is important.

The Materials

Chalk or marker board, marker or chalk, and pointer

Preparation

On a chalk or marker board, write "Keep your tongue from evil and your lips from speaking lies" (Psalm 34:13).

Directions

Read the story aloud to the class. When you get to the Bible verse, point to the board. The children stand up, say the verse together, and sit back down.

Let's Begin

Jesus had gone back to heaven. It was an exciting time because the church had just gotten started. Three thousand people became believers in one day! Close your eyes and try to imagine three thousand people. That many people would fill a football field! That's a lot of new Christians that had to learn to *(Point.)* **"Keep your tongue from evil and your lips from speaking lies."** Because the church was growing so fast, it made somebody angry. Do you know who that could be?

Satan knows that Psalm 34:13 says, *(Point.)* **"Keep your tongue from evil and your lips from speaking lies."** One of his tricks is to get us to speak evil and tell lies to each other. If Satan could get Christians to do that, imagine how fast a new church would crumble. Peter knew this. He was the pastor of a new church.

He knew it was important to *(Point.)* **"Keep your tongue from evil and your lips from speaking lies."**

Now, one man was so happy to become a new Christian that he sold a field he owned and brought all the money to Peter. He said, "Here, use this money for anyone in our church who has a need."

A husband and wife heard about this and thought, "We want people to think that we are great givers too!" The man's name was Ananias and the wife's name was Sapphira. They went home and sold some of their land. "Look, Sapphira, I got five hundred denarii for that little briar patch! Now, we'll have something to give to church too!" Ananias exclaimed proudly.

He couldn't wait to have other people pat him on the back and say, "Way to go, Ananias!"

His wife said, "Well done, my husband!" Then she thought a little longer and said, "I know that the Bible says *(Point.)* **'Keep your tongue from evil and your lips from speaking lies,'** but let's keep some of that money for ourselves. Do you think I could have just fifty of those denarii for a silk tunic I saw at the market? No one would have to know about it."

"I-I guess so," Ananias agreed. "And I'll keep one hundred denarii for myself for a new donkey. After all, it is our money, and we can do with it whatever we like, right?"

"That's right," his wife nodded.

The next day, Ananias took the bag of three hundred and fifty denarii to Peter. He made sure that all the apostles were there to see how generous he was being.

"Here, Peter," Ananias said in a loud voice. "Here are three hundred and fifty denarii that I would like to give. I, too, have sold a field.

Peter said, "Ananias, how is it that Satan has so filled your heart that you have lied to the Holy Spirit and kept for yourself some of the money? Didn't the land belong to you before you sold it, and after you sold the land, wasn't the money still yours? Don't you know that God's word says, *(Point.)* **"Keep your tongue from evil and your lips from speaking lies?"** You have not lied to men but to God.

When Ananias heard this, he fell down and died, just like that! Everyone in the temple courts froze with terror. They could hardly move or talk. Finally, a few men came forward, wrapped up Ananias' body, carried him out, and buried him.

Now, Sapphira didn't know what had happened to her husband. She had rushed off to the market that morning and bought the silk tunic. She put on her makeup and best jewelry. She wanted everyone to see what a generous, gorgeous woman she was. Sapphira strolled up to the temple and strutted up to Peter. Everyone was looking at her, but no one spoke a word. I must really be impressing them, she thought.

Peter said, "Did you get three hundred and fifty denarii for the land you sold?"

"Yes," Sapphira answered, tossing her head back. "That is the price."

Peter said to her, "You know that you should *(Point.)* **'Keep your tongue from evil and your lips from speaking lies.'** Look! The men who just buried your husband are at the door, and they will carry you out also."

At that moment, Sapphira fell down and died, just like that! And sure enough those same young men carried her out and buried her beside her husband. Great fear grabbed the whole church. They realized that God is serious when he says *(Point.)* **"Keep your tongue from evil and your lips from speaking lies."**

Questions

- Why did Ananias and Sapphira lie?
- Tell about a time when you were tempted to lie.
- How can you "Keep your tongue from evil and your lips from speaking lies"?

Story Extension

- Have the kids make this simple craft. Snip the back of an envelope from top to bottom. Lick and seal the flap. Bend it so it resembles a mouth. Draw teeth and a tongue on the inside and lips on the outside. On the inside, write, "Keep your tongue from evil." On the outside write, "and your lips from speaking lies." Psalm 34:13. Put your hand in the "mouth." Make it open and close while the verse is repeated.

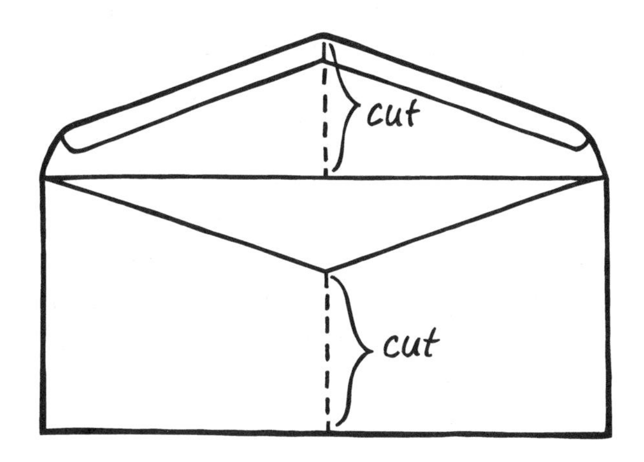

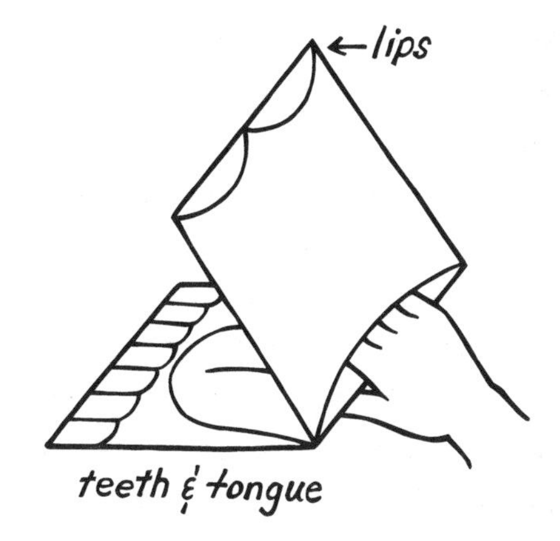

- Use vanilla wafers to represent lips. Spread chocolate or vanilla frosting between two cookies. Use a slice of strawberry to resemble a tongue. These taste delicious and that's no lie!

Other Story Possibilities

- It's easy to intersperse Scripture into Bible stories. "Encourage one another and build each other up" (1 Thessalonians. 5:11) can be inserted into stories about Barnabas. You may find these in Acts 4:36, 9:27, and 11–15.
- The verse "For all have sinned and fall short of the glory of God (Romans 3:23) lends itself well to the story of Adam and Eve and the fall of man.

4-5

Modern-Day Monologue

Imagine what life would be like if Jesus walked into the twenty-first century. What would the infant Christian church look like in the new millennium? In this modern day monologue, Philip encounters the Ethiopian who has been transformed into a treasurer for a Middle Eastern businessman. Philip joins him in his limousine to share the good news. The children will learn that the Gospel is as exciting today as when Jesus trod the earth.

The Story

Philip and the Ethiopian, Acts 8:26-40

The Point

Following Jesus is exciting.

Materials

Modern-day clothes

Preparation

Dress in a casual modern-day outfit, such as jeans and shirt. Practice the script a few times before you read it to the class.

Directions

Gather the children around as you sit in the middle of the room. It would add to the impact of the story if it were memorized.

Let's Begin

Hey, there, my name is Phil Alan Thropist, but you can call me Philip. I gotta tell you what happened to me the other day. I was loading my van with canned food to take to our church's food pantry. Next thing I knew, a man picked up a crate of cans and was working beside me. He said to me, "Go south on I-95 that takes you into Las Vegas." I turned around to ask who he was or why he wanted me to go there but he was...gone...poof...gone! I dropped all my cans, and I began to understand...that was no man, but an angel of the Lord.

Now this may sound way weird to you, but I've kind of gotten used to being surprised by God. Man, life has been one nonstop roller coaster adventure since I became a Christian! I don't even question God's directions for me anymore. I just go. So I hopped in my van and headed toward Vegas.

I was running out of gas and pulled into this little gas station in the middle of Nowhere, USA. Nothing out here but cacti and tumble-weed. As I was filling up, this shiny, black limousine pulls up. Wow, it was something! That limo looked like it was two city blocks long. It stopped, and the windows all rolled down at the same time. I was close enough to catch some of that air conditioning as it rolled out. Whew, it felt good. I peered in and someone peered out. I looked past his laptop computer, entertainment center, and refrigerator. There was even a shelf in that limo stacked with books about tax laws. He was some important-looking dude, all decked out in gold chains and a business suit. He was wearing a turban. He lowered his glasses and smiled.

I went in to pay for my gas. I was about to leave, but I felt like God was telling me, "Go to that limo and stay near it." So I went up to it, feeling kind of strange. I mean, what was I supposed to say to this guy? He was a complete stranger.

Well, of course, God was in charge. The man was reading. I couldn't believe my ears. Although he had a heavy accent, I could tell he was reading the Bible out loud.

Now, when God opens a door, you only have one choice—walk through it. I asked the man, "Do you understand what you're reading?"

He shrugged his shoulders and said, "How can I understand unless someone explains it to me?" Right then I knew, beyond a shadow of a doubt, what I was doing out here at this forgotten little gas station.

"I might be able to help you," I said, and reached out my hand to introduce myself.

He said, "My name is Aziz Nebuah. I am the treasurer for a large business in my country. Come, please. Tell me of this book which I do not understand."

I climbed into that air-conditioned limo. Ahh. He just happened to have his Bible open to Isaiah 53. Aziz only had the Old Testament. So we started right there. It read, "He was led like a sheep to the slaughter, and as a lamb before her shearers is silent, so he did not open his mouth..."

"Who is this speaking of?" Aziz asked. His eyes told me he really wanted to know.

I had the unspeakable privilege of introducing Aziz to Jesus Christ. I told him that Jesus is the Lamb of God and that he died for our sins. Jesus silently took the punishment that we deserve because he was the sacrifice for our sins. I also told Aziz that Jesus is my best friend and Lord.

I don't know how much time flew by while we sat there and talked, but the fire in that man's eyes was contagious. It was like some heavy blanket that had been blinding him was thrown off and he could see! Aziz was so excited he said, "Look, there's some water. I do want to get baptized today. Now."

Why not? I asked the gas station owner if we could use his little pond out back for a baptism. He just stared at me and said, "Uh, I reckon so." Two ducks waddled off as we stood there in the muddy water.

I said, "Do you believe with all your heart that Jesus is the Christ?"

"Yes," Aziz said, "I believe that Jesus Christ is the Son of God."

Dirty water dripped down his turban, trickled through his beard, and splashed onto his waterproof watch. We laughed and splashed each other. Man, that water felt good. Aziz said he never felt cleaner. And then he left in his limo.

I stood there in the middle of the road, waving, as that long limo became nothing but a speck in a cloud of dust. I stood there dripping...dripping and smiling. My wet sneakers squeaked as I walked back to my van. Man, life without Jesus would be so boring!

Questions

- How do you think Philip felt about his encounter in the desert?
- How is Philip's call to the foreigner like your call to tell others about Jesus?
- Can you think of someone you could tell about Jesus?

Story Extension Ideas

- Have the children look up Isaiah 53 and Acts 8 to find the parallels there with the story. See if they can try to find the prophecies in Isaiah 53 that were fulfilled in Christ.
- Children will enjoy extending Aziz's story. Have the children write about his going back to his homeland and starting to share the good news with others. You can demonstrate the idea of the great commission by filling a bowl with water. Sprinkle pepper all over the surface of the water. Each pepper flake represents individual Christians. We are called to spread the cleansing news of the Gospel. Put a bar of soap in the middle of the pepper, and watch the "Christians" scatter everywhere to obey.

Other Story Possibilities

Almost any Bible Story can be transformed to our era with a little imagination.

- Levi left his riches behind to respond to Jesus' call. Let the kids write about a big-time CEO swirling in cash and living life in the fast lane when Christ calls him to full-time mission work. See Luke 5:27-31 and Mark 2:13-17.
- Compare Jonathan and David's friendship to two friends who aren't allowed to see each other because of Jonathan's father's traditions. See 1 Samuel 20.

2-5

Tour the Tale With Light

Paul's story, so profoundly revolutionary, demands to be told in a radical way! The children take a tour of the tale, the narrator lighting up each picture along the way. The story is told in the first person, present tense, to create an effect of reality. The illustrations in the book are meant to be enlarged and can even be colored by the children before the story is told. They'll be thrilled to see that their work is showcased as part of the larger story that the whole class enjoys.

The Story

Paul's Conversion, Acts 9:1-19

The Point

Jesus can change my life.

The Materials

Enlarged copies of the pictures on pages 148-149, scissors, putty, two flashlights (one to shine on the pictures and a smaller one to read the script by), chains (or keys) to rattle, rolled-up paper for letter, and crayons or markers

Preparation

Enlarge the pictures on pages 148-149, and have the children color them. If you have more children than art, let them share pages to color. After the pictures are prepared, hang them around the room with the putty (without the children watching). If possible, hang picture # 2 on the ceiling. If you can, hang the pictures far apart so the children can walk with you from one picture to the next. Have a rug available in the center of the room so the children can sit down while the lights are out.

Directions

After the pictures are hung, bring the children into the room, and have them sit on the carpet. When the kids are quiet, turn out the light and begin the tale. Keep your smaller flashlight shielded so its light doesn't ruin the effect.

Let's Begin

Hatred. Burning, bitter, blind hatred. That's what I, Saul of Tarsus, feel toward those people who believe in Jesus. Jesus Christ—that impostor! He was a mere man, but he claimed to be God in the flesh. Oohh, that makes my blood boil! How can any human being dare say he's God? How can people believe a fairy tale like that? If those followers are that stupid, they deserve what they get—death!

I've been trained as a Jew my whole life. I've gone to the best schools and have sat with the best teachers. I can't help it I'm so brilliant. I know the Scriptures inside and out, and the name of Jesus Christ isn't anywhere in those sacred books. This Christianity thing has gone too far. It must be crushed, I tell you! *(Pound the table.)* Thousands of people, even many of our priests, are starting to believe those disgusting lies about Jesus. I tell you, I will stop it! *(Pound your hand.)* These people must be destroyed before they ruin our Jewish way of life.

I'll tell you how I've helped God. I've been going from home to home and from synagogue to synagogue, dragging these believers off to jail. I don't care if they are men or women. They are beaten. They're whipped. I laugh when I hear their children cry. What kind of people are these? They refuse to curse the name of Jesus, and that drives me crazy! How does this Jesus grip them from his grave—wherever it is? How can they be so blind? I've heard that these believers are disappearing from our city, the cowards! That won't stop me! See this letter in my hand? *(Unroll letter.)* It says that I can search the synagogues in Damascus looking for these crazy Christians, put them in chains *(Rattle chains.)* and drag them home to Jerusalem to throw them in prison. And I will.

I'm leaving now. But first, let me ask you. Do any of you believe in Jesus? *(Lean forward, rattling the chains.)* I'm bringing a group of men along to help me drag home my prey. I'm mounting my horse and traveling along. Won't the chief priest and all the elders be impressed with me when I drag back scores of Christians? Ha.

Not much longer. I've traveled a hundred and fifty miles on this horse; we're almost there. It's noon.

(Shine flashlight on Picture #1.) Ahh! What's that light? I fall to the ground! Have I been struck by lightening? Has the sun fallen from the sky?

(Shine light on Picture #2, which is on the ceiling.) Sshh. What's that sound? It's coming from above. It's a voice saying, "Saul, Saul, why are you hurting me?"

"Who are you, Lord?" I ask.

"I am Jesus, whom you are harming. Now get up and go into the city, and you will be told what you must do."

(Shine light on Picture #3.) The men traveling with me stand there speechless. They say they heard a sound but did not see anyone. I get up from the ground, dazed and confused. But when I open my eyes, I can see nothing. I stumble and fall. One of my men takes my hand. And that is how I, enlightened Saul of Tarsus, enter Damascus—blind, stumbling, waving my hands in front of me. Ha!

(Turn out the flashlight.) As fast as a lightening bolt can pierce the sky, my life is changed. I've met Jesus Christ! He is the Lord of glory and I have been a fool, a murderous fool. I sit there in the darkness, blind and broken. Yet as the blackness wraps around me, for the first time in my life, I can see. I can see the truth that Jesus is the Christ, the Messiah for whom we've waited and yearned. When I thought I was so brilliant, I was truly blind, blind and lost without Jesus. I will not eat or drink for three days. All I do is pray.

(Shine light on Picture #4.) I have a dream that a man named Ananias is coming and placing

his hands on me to help me see. Maybe I'm starting to see things in my blindness. Why would God do anything good for me after what I've done to him? No Christian in his right mind would come anywhere near me.

(Shine light on Picture #5. Knock, knock.) What's that knocking? I hear a man's voice saying he is Ananias. Am I dreaming again? I hear footsteps coming closer to me. If he is a Christian, what will he do to me? Everyone knows about me. I'm scared. I'm caught. Oh, help!

(Shine light on Picture #6.) He has his hands on my…head. They should be wrapped around my throat! He is saying, "Brother Saul, the Lord—Jesus, who appeared to you on the road—has sent me so that you may see again and be filled with the Holy Spirit."

(Shine light on Picture #7.) Brother! He called me brother! And I'm still alive. My eyes! I can…SEE! I can see! I'm still alive and I can see!

(Shine light on Picture #8.) I waste no time. The very first thing I do is get baptized. Nothing comes between me and my new Lord. I eat some food and feel strength flooding back into my body. I feel new in every way! I am new—new and ready to turn the world upside down for Jesus Christ. I was blind but now I see.

Questions

- How did Jesus show his power to Saul?
- How did Saul's feelings about Jesus change?
- Tell a time when Jesus changed the way you felt about something.

Story Extension Ideas

- Photocopy the pictures at 100 percent, and have the children make a book and practice sharing the story with younger children in their own words.
- Blindfold the children, one at a time, and have them experience blindness. See if they can do anything for themselves. Make a list of their feelings, and then compare physical darkness to spiritual darkness.

Other Story Possibilities

- Almost any good picture book that you are willing to sacrifice can be told in a Tour-the-Tale-With-Light fashion. Write the words out for each picture for your own script. This works best if the illustrations are printed on only one side of the page. You may want to get two copies of a book if this is the case. One perfect book for this is called, "This is the Star" distributed by Scholastic. It tells the story of Jesus' birth in cumulative verse. It's an inexpensive yet exquisite paperback with illustrations on one side of the page. The renderings are aesthetically intriguing, setting the appropriate mood for this mode of storytelling.
- Assign portions of Psalm 23 to teams of authors and illustrators in your class. Keep the illustrations consistent in their medium and tone.

SAUL
SAUL
SAUL
1.
2.
3.
4.

5.
6.
7.
8.

K-5

Cumulative Drawing

Using a large dry-erase board, you can draw simple cumulative pictures to illustrate almost any Bible story. Children love the suspense of guessing what you are drawing, so this method leaves an impression on children. This technique can be effective for audiences of all sizes and children of all ages. With practice, older children can use this as a valuable tool for sharing their faith.

The Story

Salvation, John 3:16

The Point

Jesus saves us.

The Materials

Dry-erase board or chalkboard (a large piece of poster board will work, and the image is permanent), markers or chalk, and a life preserver with a rope. The life preserver can be made out of white poster board.

Preparation

Practice drawing this several times. An example is found on page 153. Try it aloud on one person before you present it before a large crowd. If you can draw the pictures while you are reading the text, you'll have a smoother presentation. Before you begin, pray for God's spirit to open young hearts and minds.

Directions

Simply follow the steps below. You may ask different children ahead of time to read the Scripture passages as you go along. Let them tag their Bibles with a self-adhesive tab.

Let's Begin

Let's say I fell into some deep water and I couldn't swim. How could I be saved? Well, every boat carries one of these on board. It's called a life ring or a life preserver. If I am lucky, someone will save me with this life preserver. They would throw it to me and I would grab it. This life preserver floats so it will keep me up. I won't drown.

The Bible teaches that if you believe in the Lord Jesus Christ, you will be saved. Jesus rescues us from hell and brings us into heaven when we die. Jesus is our lifesaver. Let me draw you a story to show you what I mean. *(Get out your board and begin to draw. Try not to block part of the audience with your body; ask them to move to where they can see.)*

1. Let's say that this river is like life. All of us humans are floating along, starting at the beginning of our life and floating along to the end. **(Matthew 7:13-14)** *(Draw a river flowing about ¾ of the way across the page.)*

2. There is a problem. At the end of the river, or really at the end of our life, is a waterfall, a dangerous, steep waterfall with all these jagged rocks at the bottom. Whoever falls over the waterfall will perish or be lost because of their sins. **(2 Thessalonians 1:8)** *(Draw a waterfall at the end of the river with rocks below.)*

3. God doesn't want that for you. He wants you to live in heaven with him forever. **(2 Peter 3:9)** *(Draw a bright sun in the top right-hand corner.)*

4. The Bible reminds us that we all have sinned. And what is sin? Sin is simply doing the things we shouldn't, like not sharing, hitting, being selfish, and lying. These sins are what will drag us over the waterfall to an eternity without God. **(Romans 3:23, 6:23)** *(Draw a few squiggly lines in the river to represent waves.)*

5. God has warned all of us about the waterfall through the Bible, church, parents, and teachers. Even our hearts are like a sign warning us. **(Romans 1:18, 10:18, Hebrews 9:27)** *(Draw a blank sign in the bottom half of the picture near where the waterfall begins.)*

6. But God, in his goodness, has made a way for us to be saved. That is to believe in the Lord Jesus Christ and you will be saved. **(Acts 16:31)** *(Write the verse on the sign.)*

7. There is no other way to be saved. Now, people have four choices in life. **(John 14:6)** *(Draw the numbers 1, 2, 3, and 4 at the left-hand side of the paper.)*

8. Some people read the sign and choose to ignore the waterfall. *(Write "Ignore" next to 1 and a happy face in the river.)* They say, "There is no waterfall. There is no waterfall. There is no waterfallllllllll!" **(2 Thessalonians 2:10b)** *(Draw a surprised face going over the waterfall.)*

9. Some people say, "I will be saved by the Lord Jesus Christ someday…someday." *(Draw a smiling face with eyes closed in the river, and write "Someday" next to the number 2.)* Somedayyyyyyyy! Too late. **(2 Corinthians 6:2)** *(Draw another surprised face over the waterfall.)*

10. Now, some people try to find other ways to be saved. *(Write "Other Ways" next to the number 3.)* This person here is holding onto a branch from a tree called "my friends." His friends are more important to him than pleasing God. *(Draw a tree with the words "friends" on it. Draw a happy face holding onto the tree from the river.)* Can his friends save him? No, because there is one way to be saved: *(Point to the sign you drew and let the kids repeat it with you.)* Believe in the Lord Jesus Christ and you will be saved.

11. This girl thinks that if she collects and enjoys a lot of things, she can escape the waterfall ahead. So she puts her toys and dolls and bikes and TV and video games as first place in her day and her heart. *(Draw a happy face in the river with arms clutched around stuff.)* But of course, that will not work either. *(Draw the girl over the waterfall, hands up, surprised.)*

12. Some people try to grab onto fake life preservers. This boy hangs onto one that says, "My father teaches Sunday School." *(Draw a boy in a life preserver in the river.)* Will that save him? No. **(Ephesians 2:8-9)** *(Draw him and the life preserver going over the waterfall.)*

13. This girl thinks that if she is good enough, she will escape the waterfall. She thinks she can swim upriver. Now, it is important to try to be good and please God, but we can never be good enough to save ourselves. *(Draw a girl swimming up the river.)* She also needs to believe in the Lord Jesus Christ to be saved. **(Titus 3:5)** *(Draw her also going over the waterfall.)*

14. Some people realize that there is only one way to be saved and that is *(Point to the sign and let the kids repeat it with you.)* to believe in the Lord Jesus Christ and you will be saved. So they say, "I'm sorry for my sins, Lord. Please help me!" **(Acts 4:12)** *(Draw a face with open mouth and arm up.)* And does he?

15. You bet he does. Jesus Christ came to earth to save us. We have to call to Jesus and he will save us. **(Romans 10:13)** *(Draw a hand reaching down from the sky and joining with the other hand.)*

16. Jesus rescues us from this dangerous river and brings us close to him. **(Colossians 1:13)** *(Write "Jesus" next to the number 4.)*

17. All you have to do is call to Jesus, our life preserver, and hold onto him very tightly! Will you hold onto Jesus today and for the rest of your life? I hope so. He will hold tightly to you and never let you go. **(Isaiah 49:16)**

Questions

- How do you think each of the people in this story felt?
- How are the people in the story like people today?
- What can you do to become sure that you are saved?

Story Extension Ideas

- Get a real life preserver with a sturdy rope attached. Talk to the kids about how they can be saved from sin. Have them repeat the verse "I am the way and the truth and the life. No one comes to the Father except through me" (John 14:6). Make a shoreline out of tape on the floor. Let the children hold onto the life preserver while you pull them ashore. Talk about how children can become Christians.
- Have the kids break into groups and practice drawing this cumulative tale on a piece of paper. When they feel as though they understand it well, they can share it with the class. By the time the kids have all participated, they will be prepared to share this Gospel story with friends.

Friends
Jesus Christ
1. Ignore
2. Someday
3. Other Ways
4. Jesus
Believe in the Lord Jesus Christ and you will be saved.

Other Story Possibilities

● Adapt the story of Rahab helping the spies in Jericho (Joshua 1–2) to a cumulative tale. Each brick in the wall will help the story grow. Draw the story in black except for the scarlet cord. Talk about how the "crimson thread" (the blood) saves (Joshua 1–2).

● Draw a map while you give a brief overview of Paul's missionary journeys from the book of Acts. When you end in Italy, note its boot shape, and have the kids apply Romans 10:15: "How beautiful are the feet of those who bring good news!"

Technique Index

Techniques that need little preparation

Techniques that work well with large groups

Scripture Index

Items in boldface are complete technique presentations.

Group Publishing, Inc.
Attention: Product Development
P.O. Box 481
Loveland, CO 80539
Fax: (970) 679-4370

Evaluation for *Crazy Clothesline Characters*

Please help Group Publishing, Inc. continue to provide innovative and useful resources for ministry. Please take a moment to fill out this evaluation and mail or fax it to us. Thanks!

● ● ●

1. As a whole, this book has been (circle one)

not very helpful — very helpful

1 2 3 4 5 6 7 8 9 10

2. The best things about this book:

3. Ways this book could be improved:

4. Things I will change because of this book:

5. Other books I'd like to see Group publish in the future:

6. Would you be interested in field-testing future Group products and giving us your feedback? If so, please fill in the information below:

Name ______________________________

Church Name ______________________________

Denomination ______________ Church Size ______________

Church Address ______________________________

City ______________ State ________ ZIP ________

Church Phone ______________________________

E-mail ______________________________